# Worship Innovations:
## *Easter Season Resources*

## Janet Burton

Bright, new resources to brighten your worship experiences from Lent through Easter Holy Week and Pentecost. Involve your congregation in drama and interactive worship features which bring to life the Bible persons who lived these vital events with our Lord.

**CSS Publishing Company, Lima, Ohio**

*In loving, grateful memory of*
*Pastor Charles and Ruth Hoffmeister*
*and West Side Presbyterian Church*
*of Seattle, Washington,*
*through whom the Joy of Easter*
*first dawned in my heart*
*in June, 1945*

Copyright © 2004 by
CSS Publishing Company, Inc.
Lima, Ohio

For more information about CSS Publishing Company resources, visit our website at www.csspub.com or e-mail us at custserv@csspub.com or call (800) 241-4056.

ISBN 0-7880-1993-7

# Table Of Contents

# An Introduction To
## *Easter Season Resources*

"Oh — that we might have been there that day — to see it, and hear it, and *feel* it! It must have been so real!" Hear Peter respond, "Oh — I wish that for you, too! I was there! I was there! And it was a day so awesome I cannot even describe it to you." Pentecost — the day the promised Power arrived — and who better to explain the story from Acts 2 than the man himself? All through this third volume of *Worship Innovations*, those who lived the events come back to share how it really was, how they felt, what it meant.

Easter season spans more than three months when Lent, Holy Week, and the Sundays to Pentecost are observed. Each year worship planners search for fresh resources to bring new insights into those important Sundays of the Christian calendar. Find in this volume resources to integrate into every worship event during those significant days. For the Sundays of Lent, six monologues or readings to enhance and enrich worship or vespers. For Holy Week, two complete Maundy Thursday Communion services, a choice of two Good Friday Tenebrae vespers, and an Easter Sunrise Service with children acting the resurrection events at dawn. During the seven Sundays from Easter to Pentecost, surprise guests and interactive scripture readings inspire anticipation of the great day. In this one volume there is a storehouse to supply several years of innovation for most congregations.

As noted, this is the third in a set of *Worship Innovation* volumes. In *Volume One: Hanging The Greens For Christmas*, we introduced nine original programs for that joyful event, along with five plans for integrating the Advent wreath or candles into morning worships leading up to Christmas. Because drama is such a growing trend in contemporary worship, we added *Volume Two: Easy Bible Drama*. In that work much attention is given to the "how to's" of doing drama in the local church with non-professional actors and crew. Included are appropriate ways to use drama, enlisting a drama troupe, building a costume and prop collection, conducting rehearsals, and more. The book is specific to Bible drama, but much of the instruction applies also to the currently popular contemporary skits. With those valuable "how to's" come fifteen original Bible-based scripts, easy to produce in almost any size church.

Now in this third volume, *Worship Innovations: Easter Season Resources*, we further enrich worship with easy-to-produce monologues and readings, complete services, and scripts. The publisher generously gives permission for duplicating scripts for use on a production, making the book economical as well as useful. The *Worship Innovations* series is dedicated to providing ideas that can be implemented by lay workers and busy ministers in almost any circumstance. And with that pledge, we cheer you on to worship that may be brighter, deeper, and more inspiring than any your people have known. May you have a blessed Easter season!

Janet Burton

# Chapter 1
## The Paths To Calvary
## Six Drama Readings For Lent

**Description:** Seven personalities from Jesus' last weeks speak of their encounters with him as he journeyed to Calvary. These six short, dramatic monologues or readings are designed to be incorporated as special features in worship or vespers each week of Lent. While they are written to be costumed monologues performed live, there are other options. They would lend to being previously videotaped and shown on a large screen. More simply, they could be effective readings by costumed actors.

**Preparations Needed:** Enlist someone to act as **drama coach** to ensure these six presentations are professionally done. **Select actors** carefully, taking into consideration the personality of each Bible person to be portrayed. A committee could help in preparing **costumes and simple props** as listed in bold type below. Ministers may wish to **coordinate each worship service**, correlating the music, message, and monologue. **Two readers** are needed to introduce the drama setting, and read the scripture selections each week. Notes about the monologues and actors may be included in your **printed worship programs.** Further preparation ideas are given as appropriate throughout this chapter.

Sound and lighting **technicians** may be needed. Also a camera and cameraman, if the videotaping option is used.

**Characters Needed:**
>*First Week of Lent:* Salome, Mother of James and John
>*Second Week of Lent:* Zacchaeus, Roman Tax Commissioner
>*Third Week of Lent:* Lazarus, Whom Jesus Raised from the Dead
>*Fourth Week of Lent:* Caiaphas, Jewish High Priest
>*Fifth Week of Lent:* Nicodemus and Joseph of Arimathea, Secret Disciples
>*Sixth Week of Lent:* Judas Iscariot, Who Betrayed Him
>*Two Readers* (these may be ministers)

**Costuming and Props:** A committee may prepare the **seven costumes and simple carry-on props** needed. Suggestions are given here to provide a concept from which they can work. Consult Bible art and illustrations for authentic-looking dress ideas.

*Salome:* She needs a drab tunic of gray or olive, and sandals. Her shawl for travel could be of a plain monks cloth or undyed natural wool. Make her veil, which wraps around head and shoulders, from a two-yard length of soft black cloth. Overall, she is dressed in dismal colors, and her clothing is wrinkled from days on the road. She carries **an uneven bundle,** tied with thongs or raffia, which suggests her personal effects for the long trip from Galilee.

*Zacchaeus:* Find him a finer, striped tunic in jewel-toned fabric, belted with a contrasting sash, befitting a wealthier person. His head square is a tapestry, topped with contrasting turban. He carries a **leather money bag or satchel**, and wears sandals. Note also that he will need a **small platform** (about 3 feet square) to elevate him another 18 inches above stage level. Make this of wood, and paint it black. Set **a tall plant** on a front corner of the platform.

*Lazarus:* His tunic is of heavy, neutral, domestic fabric, belted with a slightly darker sash. He wears a head square of muted stripes, tied in back. In one arm he carries a **wide basket of melons, oranges, and grapes** for the dinner he is hosting.

*Caiaphas:* Dress him in white cotton slacks or sport pants, covered by a floor-length white tunic. Overlay these with an open black cloak. He needs a prayer shawl (large and white with corner tassels) extending over his head and shoulders to knee length. Over this place a black turban. Gold chain necklaces would suggest official-looking status. His carry-on is **a small scroll**, wrapped in tapestry and tied with gold cords. (It will not be opened.)

*Nicodemus and Joseph: (Note this is the only dialogue of the series, and may require an additional rehearsal as they familiarize themselves with the interaction.)* These members of the Jewish ruling council should be well dressed, yet not so grandly as Caiaphas, their leader. Provide both of them similar outfits beginning with black tunics. Overlay these with six-foot, fringed, white prayer stoles, which drape across their heads and shoulders and hang to knee length. Top with black turbans. Tie black scripture **phylacteries** to their upper arms and foreheads with black cords. Nicodemus carries a lighted **candle in a rustic clay holder. A wooden garden bench** is also needed. (A backless picnic bench would work.)

*Judas:* His tunic is of heavy, unbleached domestic fabric, belted with a leather strap. Tie a small bag with coins on the belt to serve as his treasury. Like Salome, he has been traveling, and his clothing is wrinkled. Over one shoulder is his travel cloak, a large poncho of brown woven fabric. His tan head square is secured with a band of faded blue fabric. He carries a **10-foot lead rope.**

**Rehearsals:** These monologues are simpler to produce than some drama scripts, because there is no interaction between actors (with the exception of the dialogue on week five). Each may rehearse separately, so schedules do not need to be coordinated; and one rehearsal for each may suffice. Consider these instructions carefully.

*For costumed, live monologues:* Enlist the cast about a month ahead. As each is recruited, read through his/her script together, talking about actions and voice inflections. Allow two weeks for an actor to memorize and internalize his script and rehearse actions privately. (Be available to help during this period, if asked.) Work with the costume and props committee during this time to assure the costumes will fit. Get together with each actor one week ahead (include lighting and sound technicians) for a dress rehearsal, and work with the part until it is ready. If needed, plan a last rehearsal during the week, or early on the day it is to be presented.

*For a videotaping and later showing: (Note: It is best not to attempt this method unless professional results can be assured.)* Go through the steps described above, with these extra considerations. Enlist a skilled camera operator with access to good equipment, and knowledgeable lighting and sound technicians. Schedule the video session after the dress rehearsals have been done, and at least a week prior to the Sunday showing. Arrange for several actors to be taped on the same day, to maximize the time of the technicians. Video each actor in turn, scheduling extra time for several "takes." Give careful attention to voice level, so the message will be clear. Depending on the equipment and level of skills available, some editing may be possible. View the product before releasing each actor, to avoid everyone's having to return at a later time for a retake. Appropriate background music could be dubbed in later.

*For readings by costumed actors:* Follow the plan above for live monologues, with these adaptations. Actors will not need to memorize scripts, but voice inflection and gestures will be even more important. The script should be secured on an attractive clip board, which can be held in one hand, leaving the second hand free for simple gesturing. Suggest that the actor stand free of a pulpit or lectern so the full effect of costume and action may be better seen.

## First Week Of Lent
## Salome, Mother Of James And John
## "The Path of Service" — Matthew 20:20-28

**First Reader:** Jesus and his disciples, with several women from Galilee, are journeying toward Jerusalem for Passover. Jesus has a growing awareness and dread of the events to come, which will lead to his crucifixion and death. The band has traveled a route along the east side of the Jordan River, south through Perea, where Jesus stopped to bless the small children. Turning west toward Jericho, they encountered the man we call the "rich young ruler," who was unable to make the sacrifices required to join Jesus' disciple group.

We join them now on the Path to Calvary, as they continue toward Jericho. Jesus calls his Twelve aside to warn them again of his impending suffering and death. Salome, mother of James and John, and the other women, are not part of that conversation. As the men rejoin the group, Salome gathers her two grown sons, John and James, and makes her request: that Jesus promise her boys the highest positions when he forms his new kingdom.

**Second Reader: Matthew 20:20-23**

**Salome:** *(She enters during the scripture reading, carrying her bundle in both arms, and shaking her head as if not understanding Jesus' reply. She speaks defensively.)* It seemed the perfect time to ask, and I thought surely Jesus would be agreeable to our request. His popularity is good — just look *(she gestures an arc toward the congregation)* at how the crowds flock to hear him, and bring him their babies for blessing. Impressive men — *(indicates to the east)* like that wealthy young ruler yesterday — are asking to join our cause. What better time could there be to talk about how the new kingdom will be organized?

*(She swings the bundle down, holding it by the strings, and pantomimes with her free hand.)* When that young man walked away so sad, all of us were puzzled. How could Jesus turn away someone with so much to offer — not just in money, but in ability? Peter even asked him, "Lord, if he isn't good enough, who can possibly be saved?" *(Drops her bundle at her feet, and rubs her forehead as though thinking. Then looks up with surprise.)* Then we realized! Maybe that young man could not give up his possessions and his life to follow; but *(pauses, gestures to the imagined disciple group)* every one of these disciples had done exactly that. Every one had given up his house, his job, his family — his life! *(Gestures, palms up.)* Surely that counts for something with God?

*(Her hands drop, and she shrugs defensively.)* Peter even asked him, "Lord, we've left everything for you. What reward will there be for us?" *(Aside.)* We all thought it, but only Peter would ask it, wouldn't you know? And Jesus' answer delighted us all! *(She steps forward a step, and points both index fingers to the congregation.)* Jesus said — are you listening? Jesus said, "You'll get a hundred times as much as you left — plus — eternal life! And ..." *(shakes one finger again)* are you listening? "And — in my glorious kingdom, you will sit on twelve thrones, judging the twelve tribes of Israel"! Twelve thrones! *(Extends her palms, asking with excitement.)* Can you just see my James and my John on thrones, judging?

*(She steps back, thoughtfully, shaking her head.)* That's why I thought it was the time to ask Jesus if my two boys could sit on the thrones nearest him. It made perfect sense to me! *(She steps back and waits, head bowed, during the reading.)*

**Second Reader: Matthew 20:24-28**

**Salome:** *(Steps forward again to speak.)* Well, that really stirred up a hornet's nest, didn't it? We were careful to ask Jesus privately — the boys and I did. But, I guess our voices carried, and — wouldn't you know, one of the others was listening. And word spread faster than you can imagine. *(Shakes her head soberly.)* Oh, were they mad at us! You would have thought we asked for the moon. We didn't mean to *(gestures)* push the others out — all the way out, at least. We just wanted to assure that James and John would sit closest to him. After all, *(hands to her chest)* we're family, you know. And *(aside)* I know I'm their mother, but — they really are the best qualified of the lot.

Well *(she gently kicks the bundle and takes a step)* Jesus' answer set us all back. And now we are wondering just what kind of a kingdom he has in mind to build. "We aren't going to take positions over each other, and have authority like the world's organizations do," he said. "But in our kingdom, the servant will be the greatest — the slave will be first." *(Shakes her head in disbelief.)* Can you figure it? The janitor being the boss? The hired hand being in charge of all the others?

*(Stooping, she picks up her bundle to leave.)* One thing I have to admit, though. Jesus may be hard to understand, but he is a gentle and kind man. And determined! There he goes — *(points toward a door)* off toward Jerusalem. It doesn't bode any good for him there, but he's set his face to go. And "go" he will — with all of us tagging right along with him. *(She starts in that direction, turning back as she speaks.)* Who knows what waits us there? *(Exits in the direction she has pointed.)*

## Second Week Of Lent
## Zacchaeus, Roman Tax Commissioner
## "The Path of Salvation" — Luke 19:1-10

**First Reader:** Jesus and his band continue on their way from Galilee to Jerusalem. After traveling south through Perea, the country east of the Jordan River, they have now turned west, on the final leg of the journey. Crossing the ford of Jordan just outside Jericho, they come into the rich, resort city of dates and palms and royal rose gardens. Passover is near, and crowds are thick on the roads. Caravans of camels and donkeys share space with religious pilgrims, local merchants, Roman soldiers, and the citizenry.

At every entry of the city sits one of Rome's hated — the local tax collector — demanding his due for merchandise, crops, carts, animals — indeed for the privilege of living in the Empire! Impatience mixes with sweat and dust and tropical heat. And somewhere in the crowd, a short, pushy man is making his way, trying vainly to dodge the angry elbows of those who recognize him. Of all the hated, Zacchaeus is chief, for these persistently prying tax collectors are *his* men. He is the commissioner — the Roman pawn — the traitor who brokers the jobs for those who would sell their neighbors to feed the Empire.

**Second Reader:** Luke 19:1-4

**Zacchaeus:** *(Entering during the scripture reading, he totes his leather satchel, and climbs up on the box platform with some difficulty. He pulls back a branch of the tall plant as he speaks.)* Whew! What a day in this River City! At least there is some breathing room up here. *(Shakes an angry fist at an imaginary person below him.)* Hey! Watch where you poke that staff, mister! *(Pushes it away.)* You're gonna get somebody's eyeball! *(To himself.)* Riff raff! Foreign opportunists! Gentile dogs! These feast day crowds will take everything they can get away with!

*(Looks down the road, shading his eyes against the late day sun.)* Now where in all this tangled humanity am I to find this Jesus person? And can he possibly be worth all the trouble it has taken me to get here? If he's headed for Jerusalem, he clearly has to come this way. It's all the talk around town. They say he actually healed old blind Bartimaeus *(gestures in opposite direction of audience)* on the other side of town — just this morning. I'll just have to wait and see it with my own eyes. If he healed him, that old beggar will have to get out and get a *real* job for the first time in his life! And he's in Zeb's tax precinct. *(Shifts his satchel from one shoulder to the other and nods knowingly.)* You can bet we'll be watching for that!

And, they say Matthew is traveling with him — one of his men. Old Matthew! *(Shakes his head.)* Now what would make a man leave a lucrative booth like his in Capernaum — a highway booth, in fact — to follow a drifter like Jesus? *(He picks a twig from the plant and tears it into bits nervously.)* I thought better of Matthew. How could he leave his security — his favor with the Romans — to follow a penniless preacher with a price on his head? I guess we'll see. *(Pauses reflectively.)* This good life does have it's downside. There are days when I'd trade it just to have one real friend. *(He freezes during the scripture reading.)*

**Second Reader: Luke 19:5-7**

**Zacchaeus:** *(Looking down, as though talking with someone below him.)* Me, Lord? You mean me? *(Jumps down to stage level and looks slightly up, as though Jesus is taller.)* But ... but ... Yes, Lord! I'd be honored to have you at my table. I live this way *(points to the right with his left arm, and shoulders his satchel)* and it's not far. *(He freezes again for the scripture.)*

**Second Reader: Luke 19:8-10**

**Zacchaeus:** *(Drops his satchel to the stage and props one knee on the platform, shaking his head.)* Salvation? Salvation! Imagine — a sinful man like me, finding salvation in one short afternoon!

*(Looks amazed, shaking his head.)* I can't believe I promised all that — I mean, about giving half my wealth away, and paying back what I overcharged folks. *(Looks to his left, as though reminded by someone.)* Four times? Did I say I'd repay four times more than I took? *(Shakes his head, then nods decisively, shaking a hand for emphasis.)* Okay! Okay! I'll do it! I'll do just what I said! This Jesus — I think he made an honest man out of this old boy today. I guess I was one of those "lost" ones he came to "seek and save." *(Turns to go — then turns back with a grin.)* But, I bet I'm the only one he shook out of a tree! *(Exits with satchel.)*

### Third Week Of Lent
### Lazarus, Whom Jesus Raised From The Dead
### "The Path of Life" — John 11:55—12:11

**First Reader:** Topping a rise on the steep path up from Jericho toward Jerusalem, Jesus and his band can see the hills of the great city, and the welcome gleam of sunlight on the marble and golden Temple, with fortress and palaces beyond. There will be no unused bed in Jerusalem this night, for the city has swelled by hundreds of thousands for Passover holiday. By prearrangement, Jesus and his party stop short of the city, in the village of Bethany, and turn in at the home of their good friends Martha, Mary, and Lazarus. A welcome always awaits them there.

This night even more so. A feast has been prepared by the villagers — a feast of thanksgiving and joy. For only months before, Jesus had come and restored the life of their neighbor and friend, Lazarus, in the most astounding miracle of all. And this is the night to say thank you and to celebrate life. So, in the shadow of the city which has put a price on his head, Jesus draws strength from his friends.

**Second Reader: John 11:55—12:3**

**Lazarus:** *(He walks in carrying a large basket of melons, oranges, and grapes on one hip, and stops to look up at the stars.)* What a night! I had to come out to get a breath of fresh air. That perfume my sister just poured all over the Master's head and feet has totally overcome us all! *(He coughs gently.)* The court was already so full of guests and onlookers we could barely move. Now we can hardly breathe.

12

It's a perfect night! I tell you, *(he shifts the heavy basket and gestures to the sky)* the weather is perfect, all my friends are here, Martha's dinner was wonderful — as always, and Mary topped it off by giving Jesus this most expensive and fragrant gift.

*(Takes a few steps toward a railing or planter, and rests the basket on one knee.)* She was saving it, you know — the nard oil, I mean. It's been in the family since we were children. *(Laughs.)* She didn't even use it on me when I died! That should tell you how deep her love for Jesus is! We all feel that way. Martha and I were totally happy that she spent it all on the Lord on this one special night. We could never give a gift to Jesus large enough to pay him for what he gave to me — to us — when he gave me back my life. A man just can't put a price on life! *(He freezes through the scripture reading.)*

**Second Reader: John 12:4-8**

**Lazarus:** *(He shifts the basket again.)* Of course, Judas had to almost ruin it all. And he had a point — the nard could have been sold, and the price used for benevolent causes. God knows there are enough hungry people in the city *(gestures toward the east)* who would have been happy to share its worth. But we *do* give to the poor. Every good Jew gives alms. This was different.

*(He shifts positions slightly to free the other hand.)* Jesus understood, as always, and defended Mary's lavish gift of love to her Lord. There has always been such a bond between those two — Mary and Jesus. They seem to understand one another to a depth most of us cannot share. He says she did it for his burial. Burial? *(Shakes his head, rejecting the idea.)* How can the one who gave life to me, himself be planning to die? He *is* Life! He told us so!

And, Jesus has never been more popular than he is now. Why — *(gestures toward the party hall)* those people in there — they are talking about making him king in the place of Herod. They even want to make a celebrity of *me*, and I've done nothing but be a friend to Jesus. *(Shakes his head again.)* No, Jesus! This is no time to die! This party is just getting started! *(He exits as the last scripture is being read.)*

**Second Reader: John 12:9-11**

**Fourth Week Of Lent**
**Caiaphas, Jewish High Priest**
**"The Path of Courage" — John 11 and Matthew 21**

**First Reader:** In Bethany, Jesus has been honored at a banquet by the family of Lazarus, and by his neighbors and friends. Still fragrant from Mary's lavish anointing the previous evening, Jesus and his men prepare to enter the city to begin the holiday rituals.

But at the Temple precincts in the city below, another attitude prevails. The Sanhedrin, Supreme Court of the Jews, has met and put a price on Jesus' head. Indignant over the miracle they cannot explain away — the raising of Lazarus from the dead — and fearful

13

they may lose power over the people, this influential court has called for the arrest and death of the man from Galilee.

**Second Reader: John 11:45-48, 55-57**

**Caiaphas:** *(Enters briskly with a scroll in one hand, and speaks angrily, as though to his colleagues on the court.)* We are spinning our wheels, I tell you! The whole world is on its way to Bethany to see him do another of his religious tricks, and all we do is wring our holy hands and discuss it!

*(Points rudely with the scroll as he speaks.)* Dunces! You should have listened to Father Annas and to me when we told you to have him executed for treason. Unless we sacrifice this trouble-maker, the entire nation could turn against us, and all will be lost to the Romans. Our land — our positions — our influence — our way of life — everything we have given our lives for. We stand to lose it all — because of one uneducated pretender. *(He turns his back to the audience, during the reading of the scripture.)*

**Second Reader: Matthew 21:1-3, 6-15**

**Caiaphas:** *(Now angrier — almost ranting, pointing with the scroll for emphasis.)* The Temple! He took over my Temple! It wasn't enough that he came riding into town, masquerading as a conquering hero! No! He rode right up to the very porch of this sacred hall, and disrupted our legitimate booths and businesses as if he owned them! We lost who knows how much revenue. And I demand to know, by whose authority did he do such bodacious acts? Surely not by mine — or by Annas's.

*(Pacing back and forth, holding the scroll with both hands.)* My God! The man has courage! He has to know there is a price on his head. You would think he'd come in disguise, and stay in the shadows of the columns. But, no! He rode right up like a hero!

*(Soberly.)* And, we couldn't touch him. No one dared. The crowds are duped — mesmerized — catatonic! The guards were paralyzed against him. Listen! Listen! *(Places the scroll behind one ear and leans to catch the sound.)* You can still hear them singing and quoting the holy writings to him! Blasphemy! Pure blasphemy! Oh — *(shakes a fist defiantly)* this Jesus must go! I tell you — when this feast is over — this Jesus imposter must die! *(He turns abruptly and strides to exit.)*

<br>

**Fifth Week Of Lent**
**Nicodemus And Joseph, Secret Disciples**
**"The Path of Discipleship" — John 12:37-43**

**First Reader:** Outside, in the streets of Jerusalem, the crowds around Jesus grow larger and more vocal. Many acclaim him the Messiah, the Son of David. Some wish him to become King of the Jewish nation. Children sing Messianic praises as he passes on the way.

But inside the high court, the Sanhedrin are obsessed with how to have him arrested, condemned, and executed. Does anyone on the inside speak to defend Jesus? Do any try to turn the Council toward a more moderate plan? The scriptures tell us, "Many of the rulers believed in him — but secretly."

**Second Reader: John 12:37-43**

**First Reader:** In a garden on the outskirts of the city, Joseph, one of the Council, is standing, having his evening prayers. Quietly his friend enters and calls to him.

**Nicodemus:** *(Entering from behind Joseph, carrying a lighted candle in a shallow clay dish.)* Joseph?

**Joseph:** *(He is standing, back to the audience and hands lifted in prayer, but turns as he hears his name. There is a wooden bench beside him.)* Nicodemus, shalom! *(The two meet and embrace in greeting.)* Thank you for meeting me here, my brother.

**Nicodemus:** Shalom, Friend. *(Gestures about.)* This is a lovely garden. Is this your family's sepulcher?

**Joseph:** Actually, *(points behind them)* the tomb is new. We'll need it some day — maybe soon. The old ones, God bless them, will not live much longer.

**Nicodemus:** I would have guessed you would bury your people in the Arimathea area.

**Joseph:** *(Shakes his head slightly.)* No — we are nearly all living here now. This place came available, and we decided to buy. For now, it is a restful diversion for Naomi and me. We love to garden, and we come here often to restore our spirits. This city life is not really for us.

But, *(gestures for them to be seated on the bench)* we must speak about this situation with Jesus that is developing rapidly in the Council. Caiaphas is bent on destroying him, and *(wringing his hands anxiously)* I'm growing more and more uneasy with my silence.

**Nicodemus:** *(Touches his friend's shoulder, then drops his hand futilely.)* I share your concern, Joseph. Every day I fight the urge to speak in his defense. I find myself searching the faces of the Council, wondering how many would stand with us if we spoke out for him.

**Joseph:** *(Nods with understanding.)* On the one hand, we have everything to lose by revealing our sympathy with Jesus. We will be out of the Council — out of the synagogue — out of all polite Jewish company — the moment we declare. *(Guardedly.)* We could even lose our lives. *(Pauses, searching the evening sky.)*

And I had hoped, by remaining secret followers, the day might come when we could be influential in turning the tide in Jesus' favor.

**Nicodemus:** *(Nods agreement, studying the candle.)* I too, Friend. But things may not be moving that way.

On the other hand, the man has great powers. Look at all those he has rescued from diseases and demons — even death. Surely he can save himself without our humble intervention.

**Joseph:** *(Nods.)* One would think so.

**Nicodemus:** I was hoping he would make his move — *(gestures a wide arc)* and take over the kingdom — even before now.

**Joseph:** *(Nods again.)* I had hoped for that, too. But not so.

Back to what you mentioned — the numbers who believe he is from God, as we do — I suspect there are several. I see them listening intently as he teaches in the Temple courts each day. He makes so much sense! But there may not be enough votes to acquit.

**Nicodemus:** *(Shakes his head, running his finger absently around the rim of the candle dish.)* I don't know how to advise you, my friend. Perhaps we have time. Caiaphas and Father Annas will not act this week with the feast so near.

**Joseph:** *(Nods and pats his friend's shoulder comfortingly.)* They would not dare act now. Jesus' popularity with the crowds is so high, it would spark a riot for sure. Actually, I thought we were going to have one two days ago when he came riding into Caiaphas's front yard on the donkey colt. *(They laugh softly at the memory, and Nicodemus stands to go.)*

*(Looking up at his friend.)* Maybe we should just wait, and see if things grow worse. Then, as you suggest, we can try to block any vote to condemn if it comes up.

**Nicodemus:** *(Standing as he speaks.)* Yes, I think we have time. I'd rather wait a while longer. We have so much to lose by speaking out.

**Joseph:** Agreed. *(Joseph stands, they embrace, and Nicodemus turns to go, then turns back to ask.)*

**Nicodemus:** But, if we are wrong?

**Joseph:** *(Raises a hand to heaven.)* Then only God can save him.

### Sixth Week Of Lent, Palm Sunday
### Judas Iscariot, Who Betrayed Him
### "The Path of Disappointment" — Matthew 26:1-16

**First Reader:** The crowd nearly suffocates one disciple as he struggles southward from the Temple market, shouldering a lamb for tomorrow's Passover sacrifice. An animal large enough to feed thirteen men and several women is quite a load to carry — not to mention that this one has a mind of its own about the trip home. Judas has chosen to do this chore alone, and he has much churning in his mind. Turning southwest, he heads for his friend's house, where the lamb will be tethered until needed for tomorrow's hour of sacrifice.

Through the crooked streets of the lower city he trudges. Evening is coming on as he lowers the heavy lamb and fastens the lead rope securely to his neck. If he moves quickly, he can still detour to Caiaphas's palace, make his deal, and be home before anyone suspects. But what to do with this lamb in the meanwhile?

**Second Reader: Matthew 26:1-5**

**Judas:** *(Entering from stage left, holding the coiled rope in both hands, he stops to reflect, shaking his head in despair.)* It's looking more and more like I've wasted three years of my life on this Rabbi — three good years. It was a bad decision on my part, but I thought he was the one.

*(Again shaking his head, remembering.)* Things started to really fall apart for me that day in Perea, *(gestures to the east as he speaks)* when Jesus turned away that rich young nobleman who came to join our cause. He would have been such an asset to us. *(Emphasizes with a fist.)* His position and influence — his wealth — his enthusiasm. I thought, "Surely, Jesus, you can see we need men like this for our new kingdom." But, no! *(Angrier.)* No! Jesus made the requirements so steep, he could only refuse. "Sell all you have"? He didn't ask that of the others! James and John — they still own their boats. But then *(sarcastically, with a flick of the wrist)* they are kin. They get special favors — *(gestures high)* the top jobs in the kingdom. And that rich man — twice as valuable as those fishermen — *(flips his hand to the east)* he gets turned away.

*(He steps slightly forward and looks piercingly at the audience, touching his head with a finger as if figuring things out.)* And then I saw the picture. What would *I* get in Jesus' new government? Me, the only Judean among all these Galileans. What spot would Jesus save for me?

*(He moves a few steps right and steps down onto the top platform step, transferring the coiled rope to his left hand.)* And that disgusting scene at Martha's last weekend, when all that expensive nard oil was *(makes a pouring motion)* squandered by Mary on Jesus' head and feet. We *needed* the silver that perfume could have brought. Why on earth did Jesus allow such an extravagant waste? Several of us objected, but — as usual — I was the only one to speak up. And did Jesus hear me? Did he defend me? No! *(He reverses direction and shakes the rope for emphasis.)* No! He scolded me, like I was a stupid child. And defended her — *(points down with his thumb, as to a kneeling woman)* a foolish, wasteful woman. We can't build a kingdom on wisdom like that!

*(Shrugs his shoulders and steps down to floor level, pacing once more further right.)* The last straw for me was the big parade the next day, when Jesus rode into the city like a conqueror. I thought — I hoped — "Finally, finally, Jesus is ready to declare himself Messiah, and build our kingdom." *(Flailing both hands with excitement.)* The crowds were wild for him. The time was right. And when he strode up the Temple steps *(he steps up two steps and elbows an imaginary booth)* and upset the corrupt booths of Caiaphas and his kin, I thought, "Yes, Master! *(Makes a fist.)* Take control! Take control!" But did he seize the moment and take us into power? *(Shakes his head and the coiled rope in his fist.)* No! No! He turned — *(gestures the opposite way)* walked away — and went back to his foolish friends in Bethany. He threw it away! *(Gestures as if to throw the rope.)* Threw my future away, because it "wasn't his time."

*(Moves now further right, and climbs up to platform level, then turns back to speak.)* So now — it's over for me. The opportunity is gone. Jesus missed his chance. Now the

High Priest is going to have him arrested and killed — even Jesus says that! And, sure as tomorrow, the twelve of us will be dragged right along with him to Roman crosses. *(Defiantly.)* Well not *this* disciple! *I* for one plan to save my neck. I plan to declare for Caiaphas before he hangs me on a tree! This is one day the High Priest will be glad to see a disciple of Jesus.

*(Looks around, and beckons to his right.)* Hey, kid! Can you come here a minute? I wonder if you can help me? I need to run an errand. Could you watch this lamb for me about an hour? I'll be back to get him, and pay you well. *("Hands" rope to his right, and drops it.)* Don't let him get away, now. *(Pauses.)* What? *(Nods.)* Yes — he'll be sacrificed tomorrow. *(Judas exits quickly to the right, one hand tightly on his money bag.)*

**Second Reader: Matthew 26:14-16**

# Chapter 2
## Our Place At The Table
## A Service Of Drama And Communion
## For Maundy Thursday

**Description:** The congregation gathers around tables in a fellowship room for an enactment of the events preceding Christ's Last Supper, and a service of Communion. A stage area in front is prepared for the drama. To one side, a table and podium are ready for the pastor to lead Communion after the drama. Worshipers are seated around tables on which the Communion elements are laid. Each table has a designated lay leader to serve Communion at that table.

**Preparations:** Enlist three teams to make the following preparations. Further details are given in the service plans throughout this chapter.

**1. Drama Team: Eleven actors** in costume are needed for the drama feature. See "Characters Needed" and "Casting Suggestions" in the drama section below. Enlist **a drama coach** or director, **costume makers,** lighting and possibly sound **technicians** at least one month before Maundy Thursday. **Schedule rehearsals** as suggested in "Rehearsal Suggestions," also in the section, "I. Drama: Our Place At The Table," which follows.

**2. Arrangements Team:** The **stage area and props** will be central. See "Costumes and Props" and "Stage Arrangements" in the section, "I. Drama: Our Place At The Table," which follows. In addition, **tables and chairs for the congregation** must be set and decorated simply, then removed when the service is concluded. Also needed: **a podium and Communion table** for the minister. See the sections "Table Arrangements" and "Communion Table" in the section, "II. Worship and Communion" later in this program.

**3. Worship Team:** Ministers, musicians, and designated lay leaders will **conduct the Worship and Communion portions** of the service in accordance with the traditions of your individual church. A **worship program** may be printed to provide order of service, words of songs, and drama cast notes. A **lay leader is needed to serve Communion at each table.** (An interesting alternative would be to enlist the costumed disciple actors to take the lay leaders' chairs and serve Communion after the drama concludes.) Lay leaders may also read the scripture selections in the worship time.

```
┌─────────────────────────────────────────────────────────────┐
│  The Service At A Glance:                                     │
│                                                               │
│  Quiet Music                                                  │
│  Drama: "Our Place At The Table"                              │
│  Worship and Communion                                        │
│      Congregational Song: "The Communion Song"                │
│      Minister's Devotional Thoughts                           │
│      Scripture Readings                                       │
│      The Communion Service                                    │
│      Solo: "God So Loved The World"                           │
│      Benediction Chorus: "Oh, How He Loves You And Me"        │
│                                                               │
└─────────────────────────────────────────────────────────────┘
```

## I. Drama: "Our Place At The Table"

**Characters Needed:**

Peter, Andrew, James, and John,
Matthew, Thomas, Philip, and Nathaniel (Bartholomew),
Simon the Zealot, Little James (James the Less),
and Thaddaeus (Judas, not Iscariot)

**Casting Suggestions:** The personalities of the eleven will shine through the script best if men are chosen who reflect what we know of the disciples. Examples: select a Peter who is a strong leader type; an Andrew who is more gentle and fatherly; a Matthew who is older and known for business skills. In the script, Little James is the younger, smaller, humorous type; and Simon the Zealot is politically focused. Read through the script asking, "Which of our men would say something like that?" and enlist accordingly.

**Costumes and Props:** All should be in "authentic" **first century attire.** Enlist a costume committee to make new garments, or use those from your church's drama closet, or ask each actor to design his own. Provide Bible illustrations and art for ideas concerning appropriate fabrics, head dress, and foot wear. Keep foremost that these were working men without fine clothing, and avoid using new, bright-colored garments, but rather choose worn, unironed items.

The following **small props** will be needed by different actors:

**Peter:** a lighted taper; **Andrew:** a crock of water, a basin, and two towels; **John:** a basket of fruit, and decanter of grape juice; **Matthew:** leather satchel; **Little James:** large bowl of roasted lamb chunks, *(later)* bowl of salt water; **Thaddaeus:** large basket of flat bread, covered with a cloth; *(later)* bowl of parsley and bowl of apple/walnut mixture.

**Stage Arrangements:** At the front of the fellowship room set **three low tables** in a "U" arrangement, with the ends of the "U" facing toward the area where the congregation will be seated for Communion. These three drama tables should be only about 18 inches high (oriental style,) and 6 or 7 feet long. Improvise by bracing table tops (legs folded) or door slabs on sturdy bases (cement blocks work well). Secure lengths of unbleached domestic fabric for **tablecloths**, and use to cover tops and extend over bases.

**Thirteen large cushions** (about 20 by 40 inches each) need to surround the low tables, so actors may recline while eating. Make these by slip-covering large bed and sofa pillows or folded quilts, using a variety of fabrics which recall Bible times (tapestries, subdued stripes and solids, and twills. Find fabric remnants or used draperies and bed-spreads in bargain sales). Make them simple and large, without braids and trims. Space **five small candles** in saucers down the center of the tables. Place **four wine cups and a folded white napkin** at the center of the head table (where Jesus would be sitting to host, were he present). These should be of pottery, rustic glass or silver, such as early believers might have used. Try for a degree of authenticity.

**Rehearsal Suggestions:** Probably three rehearsals will be needed.

**1. Read-through/Walk-through:** Begin by having the disciple players sit in their as-signed places around the "U" of tables. Make five places at the head table, leaving the center place for Jesus (who is alluded to in the drama but does not appear) with Judas and Matthew on his right, and John and James on his left. On the outside of the table to Jesus' right, seat Simon the Zealot, Thomas, and Philip, with Nathaniel on the inside end facing Philip. On the outside of the table to Jesus' left, seat Thaddaeus, Little James, and Andrew, with Peter on the inside end facing Andrew. Note that these will be the positions they come to as they participate in the drama.

Read the entire drama portion of the script together as they sit around the "U" of tables. Read through the script two additional times, walking the actions from the beginning, helping each other with gestures and voice inflections. Ask the cast to memorize their lines before the second rehearsal.

**2. Full Rehearsal:** With all cast members present, go completely through the drama, trying not to use the script much. Work through questions and difficult places. Use strong voice projection instead of microphones, if possible. If some are having trouble memorizing lines, break into groups of three and work through lines together. Come back together and rehearse the full script again two or three more times. Alert the group to prepare for a dress rehearsal next time.

**3. Dress Rehearsal:** Have all costumes ready, and ask members to get attired. Work from Bible illustrations to get an authentic look. Be sure no T-shirt necks or pants legs show (tennis shorts make a good undergarment) and no socks are worn. Work at learn-ing to sit and recline comfortably in costume. Have all props ready (empty of perish-ables at this point). Then rehearse the drama with lights and empty props until it is ready. (Consider a final walk through on the evening of the performance, prior to wor-shipers arriving.)

**Setting: (The Fellowship Room)** Lighting is dim as worshipers arrive. Stage lighting and single, lighted candles on each of the congregation's tables will allow them to find their places. Quiet keyboard or recorded music (hymns of the cross) would be appropriate. The elements for Communion are on each table, along with worship programs, simple tablecloths and centerpieces, and a napkin for each worshiper. (See "Table Arrangements" in the section, "II. Worship and Communion.")

**(The Stage Area)** The table candles are not yet lighted, but a soft spotlight bathes the drama area. It is the evening of Passover, and Jesus has instructed the disciples to make the supper ready. Preparations are almost complete. As the disciples arrive, their conversation indicates their concerns about the Master, and their continuing competition to find status in the coming Kingdom. Peter, Andrew, and John enter together.

**Peter:** *(Carrying lighted candle, enters and begins to light the five candles on the table.)*

**Andrew:** *(Carries a large jar or crock of water on one shoulder, and an empty ceramic basin and two towels in the other arm. He sets the basin by the door, pours into it a quart or so of water, and lays the towels beside it, speaking as he works. He rests the jar beside the basin and sits back on his heels.)* I've been thinking that this is our third Passover with the Master, but the first we have been able to eat in Jerusalem. We've always been on the road somewhere before.

**John:** *(Coming in right behind Andrew with a basket of fruit and a decanter of grape juice, he sets them by the four wine cups at the host place.)* Not only the first in Jerusalem, but definitely the most tense. This city is more crowded than I have ever seen it. And, although the crowds seem to be hanging on Jesus' every word, the religious rulers are definitely watching us. It gives me a creepy feeling every time I go out on the streets.

**Andrew:** *(Standing up from his work.)* I feel that, too, John.

**Peter:** Jesus feels it too, I'm sure. He seems to be placing a great significance on this meal tonight. *(Gestures about the room.)* He really chose a good place for us. This is much finer than we usually have. Did you know he had arranged for this room, John? I was completely surprised!

**Andrew:** Really, Peter? I supposed he had taken you into his confidence about this. How did you find it?

**John:** We followed the man Jesus indicated to us. It turned out to be one of Mary's servants, and — to our amazement — he led us right here! *(Still standing near the host place.)* Do you have a seating plan for this meal, Peter? Who does Jesus want on his right and left, and around this head table? It's been a bit of a touchy subject lately.

**Peter:** Well, I thought first it should be the three of us, and probably your brother James. But then I thought — well — maybe Judas will expect to be at the head with Jesus. He's kind of a take-over guy these days, holding that purse pretty close to his chest. And maybe Matthew will want a place up front, too. And then there's Thomas. So I guess I'll find something toward this other end *(gestures toward the foot of the left table)* where I can come and go if something arises that needs tending.

**Andrew:** Good thinking! I'll sit down that way, too. I don't need an honored spot. *(Andrew and Peter move toward the foot and sit cross-legged across from each other on cushions.)*

**Matthew:** *(Arrives carrying a leather satchel, and greets the others.)* Shalom, brothers. It's looking good in here. Where are Jesus and the others? *(He moves toward the host place, selects a seat on Jesus' right hand, and lays his satchel on the table.)*

**Peter:** *(With a light-hearted tone.)* Oops! Better save that spot for Judas, Matthew. He'll expect to be next to the Lord tonight.

**Matthew:** *(Moving his satchel one more to the right.)* So he will! I'll take this next place so I can keep the lid on him if he gets too pushy. *(He reaches for a grape from the fruit basket, reclines with his left elbow on his cushion and nibbles.)* Wow, I'm getting hungry. This day-long fast is hard on old guys like me. How did the sacrifice go at the Temple this afternoon?

**John:** *(Looks at Peter and gestures for him to answer.)*

**Peter:** As you would expect. We were in the second group — the first was already full; and there must have been several hundred in our rank. Have you ever done the Passover sacrifice at the Temple, Matthew? *(Not waiting for a response.)* John or I had not, and it's pretty sobering. Those hundreds of men with their knives and lambs, all sacrificing at once when the trumpets blasted — *(shakes his head at the scene)*.

**Matthew:** I guess our lamb was approved by the Levites, then? I'm surprised they didn't find some excuse to make us trade for one of their over-priced ones.

**John:** *(Taking the seat on Jesus' left hand.)* We passed okay. Judas picked a good one for us. I'm not sure where he got it, but it was here waiting for us when we followed the man servant today. What do you make of all the Roman soldiers crawling about the city, Matthew? How many do they bring in to the garrison for these feast occasions?

*(Their conversation is interrupted when James and "Little James" come in, carrying a large bowl or platter of roasted lamb chunks. Andrew gets up to help, and directs them to set it on the center of the table.)*

**Matthew:** Well, it's James and James, with what we have all been waiting for. The sacrificial lamb. Smells good, men. Who is bringing the bread?

**James:** *(Greeting the brothers.)* Shalom, friends. The lamb is perfect, if I do say so myself. John and Peter caught us downstairs an hour ago, and put us in charge of finishing up the roasting and carving, and we've been getting hungrier and hungrier smelling the meat.

**Little James:** To respond to your question, Matthew, Thaddaeus has the bread. Our hosts were kind enough to bake a huge batch for us — enough to feed the 5,000 again! But Thad got caught downstairs, helping John Mark repair a bench his mother needs for their guests tonight. He'll be up in just a minute, I think. *(Looking around the table, then to Peter.)* Where's my place? Somewhere down here near the foot of the table, I'd guess. *(He starts toward the foot of the "U.")* I've never presumed an honor chair with this group. *(He sits beside Andrew, who greets him with a brotherly backslap. Then adds jokingly.)* Next thing, you'll be asking me to be the foot washer tonight.

**Peter:** Not a bad idea, now that you mention it. No one has volunteered for the job yet.

**Andrew:** We're all pretty honored tonight, Little James. This room is better than anything we've come to expect since we left Capernaum.

**Little James:** We always had it good at Peter's and your house, but — on the road — well, we've seen some pretty interesting places, haven't we, guys?

**James:** *(Taking the seat to John's left, and reclining on his left hand.)* It's been quite a ride these three years — quite a ride. And I tell you, I miss Capernaum and the lake shores tonight. I'd rather have these feasts with my family. This crowded city life isn't for me! I don't trust all these Romans, and these Temple leaders. It feels like everyone's out to get us.

*(Conversation is interrupted again as Thaddaeus enters with a large basket of flat bread, partially covered by a cloth. He looks for a spot for it on the table near the host chair, and John moves the fruit basket to make room. Everyone murmurs approval. John busies himself wrapping three of the flat breads in the white napkin for use during the feast. He places it beside the cups and decanter.)*

**Little James:** I told you it would feed the 5,000 again!

**Thaddaeus:** Little James, we still have the bowls to bring up. I'll need a little help. *(The two exit briefly as Simon the Zealot enters excitedly, with Thomas right behind him.)*

**Simon the Zealot:** Did you see those crowds, men? Did you see how they listened to Jesus' every word, and followed us all over the Temple this morning? *(The others nod affirmation.)* I tell you, *this - is - the - time!* This is the day Jesus has been talking about. His time has come. They are going to make him Messiah before this celebration is over — mark my words!

**Thomas:** *(Enters just behind Simon and stands with hands on hips, listening skeptically to his predictions.)* I don't know, Simon. *(Shakes his head in doubt.)* I'm not sure you have been listening between the lines. Jesus keeps saying, "No," to that. He keeps telling us it isn't going to work out that way. I think — *(he pauses briefly for emphasis)* I think he's going away somewhere, and I think we need to ask him about it tonight — after the meal.

**Peter:** *(Impetuously.)* Well — if he is, I'm going with him!

**Simon the Zealot:** *(Moving toward the host chair.)* Well, I want to sit up near him where I can hear him and ask questions. *(Takes the seat on Jesus' right, beside Matthew.)* Is this place taken? Is there a seating plan?

**John:** Well, we were saving that one for Judas. And there's Thomas, and Philip and Nathaniel are still not here. Any one of them could want it, so — suit yourself.

**Thomas:** *(Moving toward the head table.)* Take the end by Matthew, Simon. I'll take the next one. I want to hear what Jesus has to say, too. All I know is, he's not going to want us to do something rash and get the Romans all riled up during the feast. All we need *(gestures broadly as to a crowd)* is two million Jews fighting in the streets, and the Romans will shed our

24

blood. It will make today's Temple sacrifices look pale by comparison. *(Both men take their places on cushions, Simon at the end beside Matthew, and Thomas next to him.)*

*(Thaddaeus and Little James return with three large bowls between them. James carries a bowl of salt water cautiously, while Thaddaeus carries one of parsley and one of a chopped apple and walnut mixture. Nathaniel and Philip enter behind them. They move around, greeting the brothers with hugs. Little James returns to his place beside Andrew, and Thaddaeus sits between him and James.)*

**Little James:** *(To Nathaniel and Philip.)* Hey! About time you guys showed up, now that the work's all done. You been out sitting under a tree somewhere, Nathaniel?

**Nathaniel:** I'll never live that down, will I? Well, I wouldn't like to be under that fig tree Jesus cursed the other day. We saw it this morning, and it's dead as a hammer. I never saw a tree die so fast! *(He looks around the table.)* Are we the last ones again? Where's Jesus? And where's Judas? Did they have some business at the Temple? I guess we must be sitting over here on this end. *(Philip follows Nathaniel to the two remaining seats at the foot of the right table, across the "U" from Peter and Andrew.)*

**Peter:** I'm beginning to wonder about Jesus, and about Judas. It's nearly sundown, and everything is ready. I guess they'll be along any minute. *(All the disciples recline comfortably on their left elbows, feet extending away from the table, as was Jewish custom.)*

*(Spotlight dims and shifts to the pastor, and the worship and Communion service begins by candlelight. Disciples sit silently through the first song, then leave quietly as it ends.)*

## II. Worship And Communion

**Table Arrangements:** The Arrangements Team will estimate with ministers how large the worship gathering will be, and set up enough **banquet tables and chairs** to accommodate. Fan tables out in a dinner theater format, so that each table is separate, and everyone can see the stage area and pulpit. Allow wide aisles for people to move safely when chairs are occupied, and observe fire safety rules for the room. Set tables up early enough to allow **simple decorating.** White tablecloths or a facsimile make a good background for low bowls of flowers on each table. (Some prefer to use a crown of thorns around a votive candle, or a small wooden cross with a single flower, on each table as centerpiece.) A single candle will give enough light. Place a worship program and a napkin at each place. The lay leaders' chairs will need **"Reserved" signs.**

Set the **Communion elements:** Place a decanter of wine or grape juice, and a common goblet (or stack of 3-ounce clear plastic cups, depending on your tradition) on each table near the chair designated for lay leader. Place a cloth napkin with one unbroken matzoh or flat bread in a napkin beside each decanter.

**Communion Table:** The Minister will lead Communion from the front. As is your church's custom, set a decanter of wine or juice, a goblet, and a napkin with unbroken matzoh beside it for him to use. He may want a microphone. (The minister could also host one of the congregational tables as he leads everyone in the service.)

**Song:** "The Communion Song" or another traditional hymn used by your church when gathering for the Supper such as, "Here, At Your Table, Lord." (Print words in the program, which may also list the drama cast and order of service.)

**Minister's Devotional Thoughts:** So we find ourselves this somber evening sitting around the table of our Lord, contemplating how it would be to follow him through his darkest hours. We hear in his men the fear, the mistaken vying for position and status, the deep bonding of the previous years; and realize that we are also part of all Christ was, and is, and is to come. The humanity of the evening comes through as we watch — almost from the inside of that upper room. Many significant things happened on that night. Let us recall a few of them. *(Readers may be pre-selected from the designated lay leaders who head each table. If the room is not too large, let them stand and read from their tables, projecting to the entire room. Microphones may be needed.)*

**First Reader: Luke 22:1-6,** *The Betrayal*

**Second Reader: John 13:2-5, 12-15,** *Jesus Washes the Disciples' Feet*

**Third Reader: John 14:1-6,** *Jesus Speaks Comfort to His Men*

**Fourth Reader: John 13:33-35,** *The New Commandment*

**Minister:** *(According to the traditions of your congregation, begin now serving the elements of the bread and cup. The suggestion is that the Minister speak the words of institution, and the lay leaders at each table serve their groups, step by step, as he directs. To better identify with that first supper, have lay leaders demonstrate breaking the unbroken matzoh or flat bread as it is served; and pour the wine or juice at the tables. Add quiet background music as appropriate. The guide below is suggested, but should be adapted to your practice.)*

    *Reading for the Bread: Luke 22:7, 14-16, 19*

    *Prayer of Thanks for Christ's Broken Body*

    *Breaking and Serving the Bread Around Tables*

    *Reading for the Cup: Matthew 26:27-29*

    *Prayer of Thanks for Christ's Blood Shed for Us*

    *Pouring and Serving the Cup Around Tables*

**Solo:** "God So Loved The World" or "In Remembrance Of Me"

**Benediction Chorus:** "Oh, How He Loves You And Me," or "Amazing Grace" *(The congregation leaves quietly by candlelight as soft music continues.)*

# Chapter 3
# A Passover To Remember
# Passover And Lord's Supper Observance
# For Maundy Thursday

**Description:** The congregation gathers around tables in a fellowship room on Thursday evening of Holy Week to experience a modified Passover Seder meal, with the observance of Jesus' Last Supper. The meal is led and served by the minister and deacons, with emphasis on a deeper understanding of the Communion rite established by Christ on his last evening with his disciples.

**Preparations:** Three teams are needed: one to prepare the Passover meal, a second to arrange for the tables and Passover centerpieces, and a third to plan the worship elements of music and narration.

**1. Passover Meal Team:** Although the Seder meal has several items to prepare, worshipers on this occasion will need **only a taste** of each. The menu traditionally includes roasted lamb, hard-cooked eggs, fresh parsley, bitter radishes, apple and walnut sauce, Jewish matzohs, and red grape juice or wine for each person. (Note: The Law prescribed only the roasted lamb, bitter herbs/radishes, and unleavened bread. The other items, which have been added by Jewish culture over time, are optional.)

*Portions:* A large (4-6 pounds) lamb roast, cooled and cut into bite-sized cubes, will serve 50-60 people taking only one bite each. Only one or two sliced eggs will serve a table. One apple, peeled, finely diced, and mixed with chopped walnuts and a little grape juice, will serve a table. (Applesauce can be substituted, adding the chopped nuts.) Two sprigs of fresh parsley and a few slices of bitter radish are needed for each person. Three whole Jewish matzohs, wrapped in a clean white napkin, are required per table. Red grape juice or wine should be diluted one part to two parts water. Each person will need about 8-10 ounces (diluted measure) because cups are filled four times.

Prepare food early on Thursday, making one large plate with the meat, eggs, radish, parsley, and small bowl of apple mixture per table. Cover and refrigerate plates so they can be served quickly in the evening. Mix the juice or wine in large pitchers or decanters.

*Setting:* Although the orthodox Jewish family would use their best dishes and linens, consider serving the congregation more simply. A clear plastic dessert plate and fork, a clear 3-ounce cup and dinner napkin are needed at each place. Each table has two additional needs. Two small bowls of very salty water on either end of the table will be used to dip the parsley. A basin or larger bowl of water and towel allows for ceremonial hand washing.

**2. Table Arrangements Team: Banquet tables and chairs** are needed, one table for each 8 to 10 worshipers and leaders. Fan tables out **dinner-theater style**, and separate them so that everyone can see the minister and musicians as they lead the service. Cover tables with white cloths. In the center of each, place an empty stemmed goblet (Elijah's cup), two tall candles with matchbook, and several stems or a bowl of fresh flowers (these to be placed just before worshipers arrive). **Room lighting** should be dim, and microphones may be needed by worship leaders.

Make plans for **a quick clean** up of the room after worship is ended and worshipers have gone.

**3. Worship Team:** The minister will lead the meal observance. **Three readers** are recommended for scripture passages. In addition, **a child (8 to 11 years)** should be coached to ask the traditional questions of the youngest reader. Enlist **musicians** and arrange for piano or keyboard as desired. Special music, perhaps by a soloist or praise team, could be included with the Lord's Supper portion of the service. Informal congregational music is suggested, but more traditional hymns may be substituted. To facilitate participation in the program, **a printed guide** should be furnished for each worshiper. (Note "The Service At A Glance" below, and the parts of the service in bold print, and include those items in the printed program.)

Place a **podium with microphone** at the front of the room. A large arrangement of spring flowers and candelabra are appropriate. The Lord's Supper **goblet and matzohs** may be placed on a special Communion table, or the minister may use the matzoh and wine on the banquet table he is hosting. (Usual Communion bread and wine are included in the Passover menu, so do not need to be prepared as for a normal observance.) **A lay leader** is needed at each banquet table to serve the worshipers at his table as the minister indicates.

---

**The Service At A Glance:**

**Quiet Music**
**Praise Chorus**
**Minister's Welcome And Introduction**
**Scripture Readings**
**Minister's Explanation Of The Seder Meal**
**Lighting The Candles**
**The Passover (Modified) Seder**
**Communion Meal**
**Benediction**

---

**Quiet Music:** A recording of Jewish praise songs, or a medley of familiar hymns of the cross

**Praise Chorus:** "Great Is The Lord" or "Holy Ground"

**Minister's Welcome and Introduction:** Tonight's Maundy Thursday observance of our Lord's Last Supper will be unique and exciting. We will travel, as Jesus and his disciples did, through the Jewish Passover meal, to better understand how and why Jesus chose that hour to initiate this most sacred ordinance which we call Communion or the Lord's Supper.

The Passover celebration, which was given first to Moses, and repeated through the generations of Jewish history, commemorates the rescuing of the Jewish slave nation from Egypt almost 1,500 years before Christ came. Following God's explicit instructions, each Jewish family slaughtered and cooked a lamb, placing some of the blood from the sacrifice on the frame of their door. When God's angel, in the severest of the punishments visited on Egypt, killed the firstborn son of each home, those houses marked with blood were spared. In the aftermath, a distraught Pharaoh allowed the Jews to leave Egypt and travel northward to their homeland. Ever after the Jews remembered the "passing over" of the death angel with a symbolic meal called Passover.

Over history the Passover meal has evolved from the simple fare of roasted lamb, bitter herbs, and unleavened bread, to a more complex menu. The original design, which was to eat the meal in travel clothes, as though preparing a hasty exit from Egypt, has accrued some lovely ritual and tradition. Today's Jewish family spends several hours at the table, instructing their children and retelling the many facets of the Passover and Jewish history. It is a sacred celebration, and our sharing it with them in a modified way is our opportunity to thank them for preserving our spiritual heritage. We will not do it exactly right — we will be somewhat selective in the interest of time, and because of our limited ability to understand "Jewishness." But we will participate with deepest respect for the occasion, and for the admirable tenacity of the Jewish people in holding to their faith. You will follow in your program and be blessed by the evening's unfolding events.

**First Reader: Exodus 12:1-11**

**Second Reader: Exodus 12:12-16**

**Third Reader: Exodus 12:29-36**

**Minister's Explanation of the Meal:** On each table this evening are the elements of the Passover supper, which we will taste together later in this service. You have heard the story from the book of Exodus, and now, as we look at the food before us, we see the story summarized.

*The Unleavened Bread:* We call it by the Jewish name, matzohs. It reminds us that God's people were instructed to leave Egypt quickly, before the bread could rise. Strict Jewish families clear their homes of all leaven and flour products the day before Passover, and eat no yeast for the seven days following. This flat bread is what we will use in our observance of the Lord's Supper, following this Seder meal.

*Roasted Lamb:* To mark the home with blood, so the death angel would pass over it, a lamb had to be sacrificed. Since earliest times, a blood sacrifice has been required by God as atonement for sin. As Christians, we see a picture of the Lamb of God, Jesus, who was to come as our sacrifice for sin. Under the New Covenant, Jesus' blood atones for our sin.

29

*Bitter Herbs:* This evening we use the radish to remind us of the bitterness of slavery, which kept the Jewish nation captive for 400 years. These three items are the original menu as prescribed to Moses on that first Passover. The remaining food items have been added by the Jews over the years. We are not certain how many of these were present on the table the night Jesus and his men observed their last Passover meal together.

*"Roasted" Egg:* This symbolizes the festive offering brought to the Temple in Jerusalem at the major feast days.

*Fresh Parsley:* Spring vegetables were always on the table as a thanksgiving for new life and the early harvest. These are dipped twice in the salt water before being eaten.

*Apple and Walnut Sauce:* To the Jewish family, this sweet sauce resembled the clay and mortar used by the slaves to build bricks for Pharaoh's projects. Jewish slave labor helped build many of the great cities of ancient Egypt. The lamb may be dipped in this sauce.

*Diluted Red Wine or Grape Juice:* Individual cups are filled four times during each Passover meal. The Jewish people used only red wine, and diluted it two parts water to one of wine. At the end of the meal, Jesus used the fourth cup to institute what we know as "The Lord's Supper."

*Salt Water:* The bowls of very salty water are reminders of the tears of the slaves during those years of oppression. The parsley is dipped twice into the salt water before being eaten.

**Lighting the Candles:** At each table a mother will now light the candles. As she does so, the host will fill juice cups with a small amount of diluted juice (not to be tasted yet). The meal now officially begins.

**The Blessing:** *(All stand and pray in unison after the candles are lighted.)*

> *"Blessed are you, O Lord our God, King of the universe, who created the fruit of the vine.*
> *"Blessed are you, O Lord our God, who has chosen us for your service from among the nations, exalting us by making us holy through your commandments.*
> *"Blessed are you, O Lord our God, King of the universe, who has kept us in life, who has preserved us and has enabled us to reach this season."*
> *(Worshipers are seated.)*

**Drinking the First Cup**

**Washing Hands:** *(By the host only. At this time the head of the table dips his hands in the basin of water, and turns fingers upward, allowing water to drip off his elbows.)*

**Washing the Spring Vegetables:** *(Guests take sprigs of fresh parsley, dip them twice in the bowls of salty water, and eat them as an appetizer, thankful to God for his bounty.)*

**Breaking the Middle Matzoh:** *(The host uncovers the three whole matzohs, wrapped in a clean napkin, and breaks the middle one in half. Half is set aside for "dessert" at the end of the meal. The Minister may note that this reserved half of the middle matzoh is what Jesus used to institute the Lord's Supper. The other half is returned to the napkin.)*

**The Four Questions:** *(A young child who has been coached will come to the Minister and ask the questions so all can hear. The minister answers, by way of instructing the children.)*

> *Child: Why is this night different from all other nights?*

> *Answer: On this night the Jewish people remember their ancestors and their deliverance from slavery.*

> *Child: Why do we eat only unleavened bread on this night?*

> *Answer: The Jewish people must not eat leavened bread for seven days during Passover.*

> *Child: Why do we eat only bitter herbs on this night?*

> *Answer: On this night the Jewish people remember the bitterness of the slavery of their ancestors.*

> *Child: Why do we dip into salt water twice on this night?*

> *Answer: On this night we remember the tears of the Jewish ancestors who were slaves in Egypt.*

**First Reader: Psalm 113**

**Second Reader: Psalm 114**

**Drinking the Second Cup:** *(The minister instructs each host to fill the cups at his table. Each table then drinks the second cup of diluted wine or juice.)*

**Washing of Hands:** *(The host now carries the basin and towel to each guest at his table, allowing each to dip fingers and raise them to cause the water to run down arms.)*

**The Bitter Herbs:** *(The host now breaks the top matzoh, and the first half of the middle matzoh, and distributes pieces of these with slices of radish to each guest.)*

**Eating the Meal:** *(The minister asks hosts to pass the Seder plate at each table, encouraging each person present to taste a bite of each of the foods, reminding each other of their significance to Jewish history. The hosts will also break the bottom of the three matzohs and serve a piece to each guest with the meal.)*

**Drinking the Third Cup:** *(Again the minister instructs hosts to fill the cups around their tables, and each table drinks the third cup together.)*

**Welcoming Elijah:** *(The minister explains)* The Jewish people believed that, before their Messiah could come, the Prophet Elijah must return to prepare the way for him. At this time in the meal, the person closest to the door would open it, and leave it open, so that Elijah might enter. *(Ask someone near a door to do that now.)* Sometimes an empty chair was set for Elijah at the table. The empty goblet in the center of the table is called "Elijah's goblet." All this is done to keep the hope of a Messiah alive among the faithful Jewish people.

**Third Reader: Malachi 3:1-4** *(The door may be closed.)*

**Filling the Fourth Cup:** *(The Minister explains while hosts fill cups around the table.)* This is thought to be the time in the meal when Jesus instituted the first Lord's Supper. Rather than drink this fourth cup, which concludes the meal, and sing the traditional Jewish benediction hymn, which is in Psalm 116-118, we will wait and follow what we believe to be Jesus' innovation, the supper of the New Covenant.

**Quiet Music:** *(Accompanist plays softly as appropriate during the Communion service which follows. Special music may also be added here. The minister may also note that this is the point in the meal when Jesus may have carried the basin around to his men, washing their feet as a humble servant would do.)*

**First Reader: Matthew 26:17-19**

**Second Reader: Matthew 26:20-26**

**Prayer of Thanks for the Bread, symbol of the Body of Christ**

**Passing of the Bread:** *(Following the example of the minister, each host breaks the reserved second half of the middle matzoh and gives a portion to each person at the table who wishes to partake of the ordinance.)*

**Third Reader: Matthew 26:27-30**

**Prayer of Thanks for the Cup, symbol of the Blood of Christ**

**Drinking the Fourth Cup:** *(The minister pours juice into an empty goblet, illustrating Jesus' words. Each host raises his cup, and worshipers follow, drinking the last cup.)*

**Passover Benediction: Psalm 116:12-14; Psalm 118:1-4**

**Benediction Song:** "My Jesus, I Love Thee" (verses 1 and 2) *(Worshipers leave as the song is completed.)*

# Chapter 4
# A Growing Darkness
# A Tenebrae Service With Drama For Good Friday

**Description:** The congregation gathers on Friday in the late afternoon or evening, in a candle-lighted worship area. The service follows the somber and ancient custom of extinguishing candles to commemorate the death of Christ and the darkness of that day. A long table with seven candles is set on the stage area, with a 15-branch candelabra standing on either side. During the first part of the service, seven readings recall the events of that historic day. The snuffing of candelabra lights, and sounds of a hammer accompany the readings. In the second part, a series of dramatic monologues allow friends of Jesus to tell his story, and extinguish the remaining seven candles. Worshipers leave in darkness to await Resurrection Day.

**Preparations:** Two teams are needed, one for worship planning and one for drama preparation. In addition to the following paragraphs, further details are given for both throughout this chapter.

**1. Worship Team:** Secure **two tall candelabra** to stand on the sides of the stage area. (See "Candelabra" below.) Between them, set **a table with benches,** resembling the Da Vinci *Lord's Supper* scene. Place **a pulpit stand** in front and to one side. Room lighting will be by candles. A dim, **adjustable spotlight** may be added, one which can be faded as each of the last seven candles is extinguished.

Enlist **two robed readers** to alternate the scripture readings. A pulpit light and microphone may be needed for the minister and readers. Enlist also the **two candle lighter/ snuffers** to wear dark clothing, and to extinguish candles during the readings. Quiet **music**, congregational songs, and two soloists are suggested. One walk through **rehearsal** for those involved (minister, readers, candle lighters, musicians) will help everyone feel comfortable with his or her place, the unaccustomed dim light, and the sound equipment, before the service begins.

**Candelabra:** Stand the two tall, 15-branch holders with white tapers on either side of the worship and stage area, as indicated above. (The type used at weddings are ideal.) By each candelabra a candle lighter stands to snuff candles as the scriptures are read. Dark attire will allow them to recede into the background. Each needs a candle lighter/ snuffer. Candelabra are lighted before worshipers arrive. As each of the first six readings is completed, both actors snuff two candles from their 15 (12 in all on each side,) and a **carpenter** sounds several hammer blows. On the seventh reading, the three remaining candles on each side are extinguished, leaving only the seven lighted pillar candles on the Lord's Supper table (and perhaps a very dim spotlight) to light the drama presentation.

**Spikes:** To involve the congregation in the crucifixion experience, have ushers hand each person a six-inch nail spike, along with an attractive **printed program**, as they arrive for worship. Prepare for the **sound effects** of hammer and spikes to alternate with the first seven readings. The sounds may be pre-recorded and played through the sound system, or struck live by a carpenter dressed in biblical attire, and working on a sturdy bench to the side of the worship area.

**2. Drama Team:** A **director and six actors** are required for this second part of the service. Note that John Mark is a teenager, and Peter has two speaking parts. A costume manager is needed to prepare **dark costumes** for each actor. **Two rehearsals** are suggested: one to walk through the script and actions, and practice voice projection; the second to perform parts in full dress with the dim lighting. Seven rough **wooden candle holders with white pillar candles** are needed for the drama table. These should be of graduating heights, with the tallest Christ Candle in the center. (The holders may be simple blocks of a 4" by 4" post.) **A goblet, matzohs, and a few ceramic dishes** are also needed for the table. (See further details in the section, "II. Drama: A Growing Darkness.")

---

**The Service At A Glance**

**I. Worship Through Remembering**
   Quiet Music
   Solo: "What Wondrous Love Is This?"
   Congregational Song
   Minister's Welcome And Introduction
   Seven Scripture Readings
   Instrumental Solo

**II. Drama: "A Growing Darkness"**
   Benediction

---

## I. Worship Through Remembering

**Quiet Music:** *(Played somberly, commemorating the death of Christ.)* "When I Survey The Wondrous Cross" and "Jesus, Keep Me Near The Cross." A recording of "Surely He Hath Borne Our Griefs" from *The Messiah* could be substituted.

**Solo:** "What Wondrous Love Is This?" *(Verses 1 and 2 only, possibly a capella.)*

**Congregational Song:** "There Is A Fountain Filled With Blood" or "The Old Rugged Cross" *(Before congregational singing, the two candle lighters together light the seven candles on the Lord's Supper table. Lighters return and stand beside their candelabra through this first part of the service holding snuffers.)*

**Minister's Welcome And Introduction:** We celebrate this evening one of the most somber of all Christian traditions, the extinguishing of the lights, as we remember the cruel and sacrificial death of our Savior on our behalf. This Tenebrae is a custom which has been observed in many forms in churches for more than 1,500 years. We Christians who live in the tradition of hope and praise, always claiming the resurrection of our Lord Jesus as our own assurance of eternal life, find it difficult to immerse ourselves in the day of his death — a day without hope — a day of great pain for our Lord and his closest friends and family. But, in order to feel the joy of Easter morning fully, we must first revisit the day of darkness — the day Christ died. Let us listen to some of the events of his final hours.

**Scripture Readings:** *(Two robed readers alternate the seven readings from the pulpit. As each reading is completed, both candle lighters snuff out two candles from their candelabra, and the carpenter strikes two blows onto a spike with his hammer. Following the seventh reading, the remaining three candles on each side are extinguished and three blows are struck.)*

**1. The Betrayal and Arrest: Matthew 26:14-16, 47-50** *(Snuff two candles on both candelabra; strike two hammer blows.)*

**2. The Arraignment: Matthew 26:57-66** *(Snuff two candles on both candelabra; strike two hammer blows.)*

**3. The Denial: Matthew 26:33-35, 69-75** *(Snuff two candles on both candelabra; strike two hammer blows.)*

**4. The Trial and Sentencing: Matthew 27:11-26** *(Snuff two candles on both candelabra; strike two hammer blows.)*

**5. The Crucifixion: Matthew 27:27-38** *(Snuff two candles on both candelabra; strike two hammer blows.)*

**6. The Prophecy Fulfilled: Psalm 22:1, 6-8, 14-18** *(Snuff two candles on both candelabra; strike two hammer blows.)*

**7. Darkness and Death: Matthew 27:54-56** *(Snuff remaining three candles on both candelabra; strike three hammer blows. Readers and candle lighters exit.)*

**Instrumental Solo:** "Were You There?" *(Two verses, somberly and without piano accompaniment. Horn, clarinet, flute, or violin suggested.)*

## II. Drama: "A Growing Darkness"

**Characters Needed:**
Mary of Bethany, Nicodemus, Thomas,
John the Apostle, Simon Peter, and a teenage John Mark

**Setting:** In a scene reminiscent of Da Vinci's *Last Supper*, **a long table** is set on the stage. **Benches** flank the ends and back side, with the front uncluttered. (Weathered wooden picnic table and benches work well.) The table is covered with lengths of unbleached domestic fabric. **A single goblet and napkin with matzoh** stand before the central host position. A few baskets and ceramic bowls, and a basin and towel, may be added to suggest Jesus and the disciples were here, but have gone away.

**Costumes:** All actors are in mourning for their Lord, and wear dark tunics (dark gray, black, olive, dull navy, or brown). Head wear and props differ, and are noted in the script below. All wear sandals on bare feet. The drab attire is designed to give greater emphasis to the words they will speak.

**Mary of Bethany:** *(Enters from left and moves across the front of the table toward right center. She carries a **small stone jar or urn** for perfume, and wears a dark tunic and a veil wound around her head and shoulders. She speaks slowly and sadly.)* I was not there, but I heard about it — the awful night when Jesus was betrayed and arrested in the garden. We had seen him several times the week before. It was the week of Passover preparations, and he spent part of it in our home.

*(Mary moves pensively to her right, staring down; then looks directly at the audience.)* Since my brother Lazarus's terrible death experience, our family has never been able to thank Jesus adequately. There just is no way to repay someone for a life brought back from the grave. Our entire village celebrated and believed. When Jesus and his followers arrived in Jerusalem about a week before Passover, *(she smiles, remembering)* Martha and I fixed dinner for them all. It was a joyous reunion, and many guests came.

For me it was a special night — a night I'll remember always. We had this urn of nard perfume *(she shows it, holding it tightly with both hands)* — a treasure that had been in our family for years. One of our most precious — certainly our most fragrant possession. As dinner drew to a close, Jesus was talking with the men around the table. I found a quiet moment to slip in beside him, *(she pantomimes the act)* and I broke the seal on the urn and poured the red oil over his precious feet.

I didn't intend to disturb, but even I was surprised at how the perfume totally filled the room. *(Gestures as she speaks, still pantomiming her actions.)* Conversation stopped. I was embarrassed, so I stooped and began to wipe his feet with my veil and my hair. *(Fumbles with the edge of her veil as she remembers.)* I guess most of the men did not know what to say, but Judas spoke up quickly. All he could talk of was the wasted money that nard could have brought to the group treasury.

*(Her voice softens and she opens the jar and breathes the lingering fragrance; then holds the empty urn to her heart.)* But Jesus was quick to defend me. He understood my devotion — my thanks — my love. I like to hope that the perfume made the terrible days ahead easier for Jesus to bear. The terrible, terrible, dark days ahead.

*(Mary steps to the right end of the table and blows out the first candle, then exits quietly to the right.)*

**Nicodemus:** *(Enters from the left and walks to the front left end of the table. Over his black tunic, he wears a white prayer shawl, with **black phylacteries** bound on his forehead and arm.)* It surely was a terrible week! For Joseph and me, meeting with the Jewish Council, it was a wrenching week. *(He pauses, remembering, and shakes his head gently.)*

That plot to arrest and kill Jesus had been brewing in the Council for months. All the time Jesus' popularity with the crowds was growing, the fear and hatred of the Pharisees was growing in kind. When Jesus raised Lazarus from the dead, the crowds went wild. *(He gestures with both hands.)* It wasn't a usual miracle you see. It couldn't be explained away, no matter how hard they tried. And the Chief Priest and Pharisees called together the Sanhedrin, and decided to *(makes a fist)* put an end to it all as soon as possible.

Unless you've experienced Jerusalem in Passover week, you cannot possibly understand the craziness. Two million Jews filled every street and alley — *(gestures widely to both sides)* — it's the biggest week of the year around here. Paranoia reigned among my brothers in the Pharisees. Joseph and I debated whether to go public about our belief that Jesus is the Messiah. *(He pauses, remembering, then shakes his head decisively.)* But it seemed to us we might be strategically positioned within the Council as secret followers, to head off the plot and protect Jesus in some way. At least — at that point — we hoped we might.

*(Nicodemus paces a few steps, then comes back, talking and gesturing.)* All week it continued between Jesus and the Council — cat and mouse, cat and mouse. Jesus entered the city in a wildly jubilant parade, *(confidently)* and strode in and took over the Temple courts. The Jews could not touch him. *(He moves to sit on the left end bench, elbow on the table.)* Every attempt to discredit Jesus with trick questions and public dialogue left the Pharisees — and even the Sadducees — in tatters. At every opportunity Jesus came up with a new parable that only thinly disguised the self-serving motives of the leaders. *(He pounds the table with his fist.)* How they hated him! *(Gestures broadly, smiling.)* And how the people loved him! The leaders dared not touch him because of the people.

But *(he rises slowly, and shakes his head in unbelief)* their answer came — unexpectedly to us all — in the man Judas Iscariot — a disillusioned disciple who sold out his master *(holds out his hand as though receiving coins)* for a slave's price in silver. Can you believe it? *(Hand to his chest.)* It caught Joseph and me completely off guard. It was the beginning of the end for Jesus — for us all. Such a sad, sad end.

*(Nicodemus turns to blow out the first candle on the left end of the table, and exits quietly back to the left.)*

**Thomas:** *(Enters from right and walks to center front of table. He wears a dark tunic, with muted, solid-color head square, topped by a dark turban, and carries **a length of coiled rope** in his left hand. His tone is very angry, and he shakes his right fist.)* Judas! Traitor! I know the Master taught us to love our enemies — but we thought he meant those on the outside. It is nearly impossible to love one who betrayed us all on inside information! One who pretended loyalty!

*(He strides to the left end of the table, shaking the coiled of rope.)* How did he ever get away with it? How did we eleven grown men miss the cues and let this happen? Why did Jesus ever make him one of the Twelve in the first place? He ate and drank with us — shared our hearts and our secrets. *(He turns and pauses, unable to take it in.)*

*(Thomas rubs his forehead with his right hand, as though easing a headache, then speaks slowly, as though thinking it out.)* I think the whole twisted betrayal formed in Judas' mind the night Mary poured out her nard on Jesus' feet. Judas was outraged — beyond reason. And in his over-reaction some of us began to suspect and question his motives. Judas held the purse for our group — and he loved money. Everyone could see that. So he was susceptible to the lure of greed and gain.

*(Slowly he walks back to the center of the table as he speaks.)* And Judas was a radical — an activist who loved power. He wanted Jesus to begin his Kingdom here and now, *(makes a fist)* to destroy Rome. To some extent, we all wanted that. But I think Judas saw the betrayal as a way to force Jesus' hand — to set up a show down in the garden. Maybe he thought Jesus would resist the Temple guards by calling down angels or something.

*(He shakes his head in bewilderment.)* Who can know what a traitor like Judas would think? At any rate — he's gone now — *(shows rope)* hanged by his own hand. *(He blows out the second candle on the right end.)* But he took our Jesus out with him. *(Exits quietly to the right.)*

**John the Apostle:** *(He enters with Peter from the right. John moves forward to the right center, but Peter sits on the right end bench. John wears a dark tunic, and light head square, secured with matching headband. Peter has a dark head square, pulled down deeply over his eyes, and carries **a small towel** in one hand. As John speaks, Peter stares at his hands and fidgets with the towel.)*

It was hard for all of us to understand. Not that I'm taking up for Judas by any means. What he did was despicable and inhuman, and he has destroyed our very lives and crushed our hearts. But this teaching of a Kingdom of another realm is a hard truth to grasp. We all struggled with it.

*(Gestures toward Peter quickly.)* Peter can back me up here — we always had an under-current of competition — maybe it was ambition — among us Twelve. *(Peter nods assent.)* We were brothers, but in any group some will emerge as leaders — just sort of float to the top over time. And the group sees those natural abilities. *(Shakes his head.)* Judas was never one of those at the top — never fully trusted — and I think he resented it more than we knew.

*(He turns profile to the audience and toward Peter.)* Where a Kingdom is concerned, there have to be positions — offices, if you will — responsibilities. I have to admit *(points to himself)* my brother James and I wanted those top spots. Even my mother tried to "politic" with Jesus for our interests. And Peter *(casts a quick look back and nods)* — he sort of looked out for Number One, too. *(Peter agrees, shaking his head in shame at the memory.)*

You would think we three — Peter, James, and myself *(gestures to include Peter)* — we should have gotten it. Especially after we saw the Master's glory on Mount Hermon that day. I can hardly describe it even now. *(Shields his face with his hand, and gestures toward the sun as he remembers.)* Jesus was so changed — so bright! Moses and Elijah so real. *(Reaches upward.)* The cloud so brilliant. God's voice so clear. We should have understood about a "Kingdom not of this world."

*(John turns back toward the left.)* But Judas went farther — he wanted "his" and he wanted it now. He couldn't wait on Jesus to work it out. He couldn't trust. He couldn't submit. So he gambled — and he lost. We all lost. *(John turns and blows out the second candle on the left end and exits to the left, speaking.)* We lost the best friend we ever had.

**Simon Peter:** *(Watches John leave, then rises slowly, folding the towel over his left arm. He continues standing beside the right end bench.)* John is right. That day on Mount Hermon should have explained it. Many things should have explained it. We can see it now — you know how hindsight works.

*(Peter transfers the towel from his left arm to his right hand.)* To me the light should have dawned on that last Thursday evening in the borrowed upper room at John Mark's house. That's when Jesus, after the dinner, took off his robe and wrapped a towel around his waist, and began to wash our feet. Like a common servant — he was washing our feet in love. *(He kneels partially by the bench, showing how it was done.)* I could hardly allow my Lord to do that. I protested *(sits back on his heels)* "No, Lord!" But he insisted. And, one by one, he cleansed us all — all, even Judas.

And then he explained — drew us a picture. *(Peter rises and gestures with the towel.)* We are all to serve each other in humility. In love. His Kingdom is a gentle way of life — teaching, loving, serving, sacrificing. Sadly, this dark world doesn't operate on those principles. That's why it opposes us. That's why they killed our Lord. *(He pauses briefly, grieving.)*

*(Brightening.)* But, we who have the spirit of Jesus within can make this Kingdom work! Jesus may be gone, but the things he taught us are truth, and they will live on. *(He picks up the third candle on the right and holds it before his face.)* His light may be gone *(blows it out softly)* but his truth is very much alive! *(Putting the candle back in its place, he sits back on the end bench, head in his hands.)*

**John Mark:** *(Enters from left before Peter finishes speaking, and walks slowly across behind the table toward the right end. He is a teenager and wears a calf-length dark tunic with no head square. As Peter sits down, Mark moves next to him, resting his hand on Peter's shoulder tenderly.)* Peter can hardly tell you about the next few hours — after supper on Passover night. His pain is still so great.

*(He walks slowly around to the front right end of the table as he speaks.)* After supper the whole group — Jesus and the eleven disciples — left our upper room and walked across the Kidron to the olive press. Jesus often went there to pray — we all knew the

place well. It was late, and I was supposed to be in bed asleep, but — well — *(he smiles, embarrassed)* I admired all those men so much, and Jesus, too — so I snuck off and followed them — uninvited.

*(He pauses, remembering, and gestures to one side.)* Jesus went off to pray, and he stayed so long the rest of us fell asleep. It must have been terrible for Jesus. I think he knew what he was about to go through. Two or three times *(he pantomimes, shaking Peter's shoulder gently)* he tried to wake the men so they could pray with him. But I don't think any of them was much help to him. Nobody suspected what would come next.

*(Mark walks more to the center front of the table.)* It must have been after midnight when Jesus woke us all up. *(He shakes Peter again.)* "Get up! Let's go! My enemies are here!" he said. And up the valley came this string of Temple guards with torches. *(He traces their trail with his finger.)* There were some Roman soldiers with them, too. We were terrified — just coming off a deep sleep and seeing all that. Peter had the sense to grab his short sword and try to fight them off. Can you see him? *(Pantomiming.)* Slashing wildly at that whole detachment of men? *(Peter, sitting and listening, shakes his head in embarrassment and drops it again. Mark eyes him.)* Well, I thought it was a brave try. I couldn't have done it.

But, it was as though Jesus knew what he had to do. He told Peter to put it away.

Two soldiers grabbed Jesus, and I — I just ran for my life! A soldier caught me and jerked off my night shirt, but I got free and ran for home — naked — and in the total darkness. *(Mark blows out the third candle on the left end, leaving only the tall Christ Candle burning, and exits to the left.)* It was really a dark night for us all.

**Simon Peter:** *(Returning to speak a second time, he walks slowly around the front of the table, toward the one remaining lighted candle, still holding the small towel.)* I wish I couldn't remember what came next. If I could rewrite that night — my own cowardice and denial — I would surely do that at any cost.

*(Shrugs at the futility of the situation.)* Everybody ran — but John and me. I don't know what John did, but I hid a safe distance away, and followed the sad parade as they led my precious Jesus to the house of that treacherous Chief Priest, Caiaphas. I wanted so much to rush them and rescue him, but my fears and confusion were too great. And security was very tight.

*(Peter takes the last candle and holds it in front of his face, studying the flame.)* From outside Caiaphas' house I heard snatches of accusations drift into the courtyard, all the time trying to appear that I was an innocent bystander, just casually warming myself by the fire. *(He passes one hand over the flame.)* But people soon figured me out — I guess I just sound like a Galilean country boy. They kept trying to link me to Jesus as an accomplice. I denied it every time, not so much to save my neck — *(nods)* it was partly that, I guess — but to try to stay near, hoping to be there if they released Jesus, so I could take him home. I couldn't believe they would kill such a good and innocent man.

*(He sets the candle back in its place.)* But — in the end — they did just that. And I couldn't change things. And as they led Jesus away, they were hitting him, and spitting on him, and yelling insults at him. It made no sense at all. And he just let them do it. "Call the angels!" I wanted to yell, but I couldn't speak out again. *(Peter wipes his brow with the towel.)* I was too weak.

As Jesus passed through the courtyard, our eyes met. *(Pantomiming.)* His look broke my heart. I knew I had let him down, and I left and ran out into the street. Dawn was breaking, but I was too angry and ashamed to see. In my soul it was totally dark. I had disappointed my best friend. *(Peter wipes his face with the towel, picks up the last lighted candle and carries it as he exits to the right. The carpenter strikes three final blows.)*

**Benediction Song:** "Oh, How He Loves You And Me" *(The congregation leaves quietly in the darkness.)*

# Chapter 5
## Seven Words To Die By
## A Tenebrae Service With Drama For Good Friday

**Description:** Late on Good Friday worshipers gather by candlelight to remember the death of the Savior. Scripture readings, music, and prayer come alive when seven who heard Jesus' final words from the cross tell their stories. Candles are extinguished as worship progresses from light to darkness.

**Preparations:** Two teams are needed, one for drama production, and one for worship planning. Further details for each team are given throughout this chapter.

**1. Worship Team:** This service alternates music, scripture, and prayer with the seven dramatic monologues. Set the **podium** for the ministers, musicians, and reader(s) to one side of the platform. (On the opposite side, the Drama Team will create a small drama set as suggested below.) Enlist **one or two readers** to do all the scripture readings. Enlist **musicians** and allow them adequate time to prepare music which fits each of the seven words. **One rehearsal** of musicians and readers with the minister will help all participants feel better prepared for the hour.

**Candles and lighting:** Following the tradition for Tenebrae services, candles are lighted early, and extinguished gradually during the service. Use either tall, white pillar candles or very long, white tapers in holders. Graduate them in height, forming a sort of pyramid, with the tallest, the "Christ Candle," in the center. Depending on the arrangement of the worship stage, they may be in **a tall candelabra, or on a table or altar.** The minister will snuff six of them, shortest to tallest, as worship proceeds. The seventh candle will not be extinguished, as it represents our hope of eternal life. A **spotlight** is suggested, and should follow the pattern of the candles, beginning fully lighted, and diminishing as each actor completes his or her part. If no spotlight is available, house lights could be dimmed in sections as the service progresses, beginning with back and side room lights, and progressing through overhead chandeliers to platform spotlights. (Instrument reading lights will need to remain on.)

**2. Drama Team:** Enlist **seven actors** as required, each to present a monologue based on one of the seven last sayings of Jesus. Prepare simple **Bible costumes and props** for each as suggested in each part below. A spotlight is suggested, which will necessitate a **technician** who attends rehearsals and can follow the action.

**Characters Needed:** The Roman Centurion, Simon of Cyrene, Jesus' Mother Mary, John the Apostle, Mary Magdalene, Pilate, and Joseph of Arimathea

**Costumes:** All but the Centurion and Pilate need dark tunics, in keeping with the mood of the day. The Centurion part requires a Roman soldier costume, available at costume rental places, or the pattern books at fabric stores. Pilate wears a white tunic trimmed in red braid, with a white stole also trimmed in red. Further details, for head and foot wear and simple props are given in the entrance instructions for each monologue. Consult Bible art and illustrations to plan and achieve an authentic look for each actor.

**Rehearsals:** Enlist actors one month ahead of the service, and hold the first rehearsal as soon as all are recruited. At least **two rehearsals** will be needed. First, **a script reading and walk through**, when actions, gestures, and voice inflections are decided. Allow several days following this for actors to memorize and put actions with their parts. Second, **a costumed rehearsal** several days before the presentation and after parts are memorized. At this time, encourage actors to help each other work out entrances and strengthen actions and voice production. The lighting technicians should be at the second rehearsal. Consider a final rehearsal early on the day of the presentation, prior to worshipers arriving.

**Drama Set:** Create **a wayside stop** for all actors to use by placing a rough wooden bench (a yard bench could work) flanked by a large grouping of plants. Position several melon-sized rocks at the base, and drape a swag over the bench using two yards of a rough fabric.

**Alternate Staging:** While the drama is written as a simple stage production, it would also work well in a congregational setting. Actors (either in costume or street clothes) can be scattered throughout the worshipers. At their appointed times, each stands and delivers his or her monologue, using voice projection or a hand-held microphone. This can personalize the experience as actors are seen as "one of us." The same number of rehearsals will be needed.

---

**The Service At A Glance:**

**Quiet Music**
**Minister's Welcome And Introduction**
**Scripture Reading**

**Word One: "Forgive"**
**Word Two: "Whosoever"**
**Word Three: "Love"**
**Word Four: "Forsaken"**
**Word Five: "Suffering"**
**Word Six: "Victory!"**
**Word Seven: "Hope"**

**Minister's Closing**
**Congregational Song**
**Benediction Prayer**

---

**Quiet Music:** "Behold The Lamb Of God" from *The Messiah* (either a recording or a solo by voice or instrument)

**Minister's Welcome And Introduction:** We gather at this Tenebrae to rehearse again the familiar events of the day our Savior died. A somberness surrounds us when we are made to think of the cross experience of our Lord on that first Good Friday. It causes us to shoulder again our sense of guilt for the sin of our lives which contributed to his sacrificial death on our behalf. Although we closely pair the crucifixion with his resurrection on the third day following, today we set aside our feelings of victory and hope, and mourn the death of our Savior. In the stories that accompany his last seven sayings, we look for deep truths to live by — and to die by. We will extinguish the candles as we move through the service, remembering the deepening darkness of the world when it's Light and Life were taken away.

**Scripture Reading: John 1:1-5, 10-11**

## Word One: "Forgive"
## The Centurion — "Father, forgive them ..."

**Congregational Song:** "Blessed Redeemer" (verses 1 and 2)

**The Scripture: Luke 23:26, 32-38**

**The Centurion:** *(Enters confidently from opposite the reader into bright spotlight wearing the attire and helmet of a Roman soldier. On his arm he carries **Jesus' bloody, homespun robe.** He speaks first to the Scripture Reader with surprise.)* "Father, forgive them?" Was he including me? I'm not responsible for this travesty — I was just doing my job! *(He turns to the audience and pauses to think about the words.)* But what a strange response from one who has just gone through the worst punishment we Romans can give a criminal.

I watched the whole thing — the trials, the devious misrepresentations of the Jews, Pilate's futile attempts to get Jesus freed — and from my point of view, I doubt this man Jesus was a criminal at all. *(He shows the robe.)* But that didn't save him from the brutal beating and cruel tortures of my men. Crucifixions are such inhuman acts, the only way they can carry out their orders is to *(brushes the episode aside)* make a joke of it all. Most of our victims play our game — they curse us, and fight us, and scream out futile revenge. The other two did that. But Jesus? "Father, forgive them, for they do not know what they are doing"?

*(He turns slightly, and rubs his chin thoughtfully, then looks at the audience.)* We knew quite well what we were doing — or, I thought we did. I thought we were bringing three more men to die on this *(gestures behind him and uphill)* infamous hill. We carried out the orders — we nailed them up and stood our watch. It's gruesome, but we do it — it's our job.

*(He removes his helmet, and runs his hands through his hair thoughtfully.)* I thought in a few days Jesus' skull would be just one more *(indicates debris on the ground)* among the litter of human remains up here, mocking the city from this hill. But he was a different kind of man. A righteous man. I think everyone could see that. And strange things

45

happened when he died — almost like the God he kept talking to took notice. *(He gestures.)* The sky turned black — the earth shook. And now I hear that we are being pressed to guard his tomb. Rumors are that he said he would come back to life in a few days. *(Shrugs.)* Nobody ever has, but I guess there is a first time. This hasn't been like any other execution I've led. Anything can happen.

*(Speaking as to his men, and beckoning with his arm and a toss of his head.)* Come on, men. This man is dead. Let's report to Pilate and get our new orders. *(He exits briskly down an aisle, through the congregation.)*

**Minister's Prayer:** *(He snuffs the first candle, the spotlight dims slightly, and he leads the congregation in prayer.)* God of all forgiveness, help us learn with the soldier the lessons of the cross today. Like our blessed Savior, who rose above his own intense suffering and injustice to speak words of mercy for his enemies, let us lay aside our hurts and grievances, and forgive those who have sinned against us. Help us to release others from the guilt of having wronged us, that our hearts may be free of malice and at peace with you. In the name of our forgiving Lord, we pray. Amen.

**Solo:** "First Word" from *The Seven Last Words Of Christ* cantata by Dubois; or the contemporary song, "Forgiven."

## Word Two: "Whosoever"
## Simon of Cyrene — "Today you will be with me in paradise"

**Congregational Song:** "Christ Receiveth Sinful Men" or "There Is A Fountain"

**The Scripture: Luke 23:39-43**

**Simon of Cyrene:** *(He enters on floor level from the left side of the worship room, and crosses in front of worshipers. The spotlight is slightly diminished from the first speaker. He wears the tunic, turban, and over cloak or poncho of a traveler, with sandals, and has a satchel slung over one shoulder. In his hand is **an empty crown of thorns**, which he picked up from the foot of Jesus' cross. Stopping by the bench, he slumps down on it.)* That day turned my life upside down! Have you ever had a day like that — when you were going about your business and something just *(pantomimes)* jerked you away and changed it all?

I'm not in Jerusalem very often — it's quite a trip *(gestures southwest)* from North Africa, you know — by boat and by foot. But like thousands of others, I had come for the Passover, as instructed in our Law. Lodging was non-existent, and I had stayed out in the countryside with friends. *(He slings down his satchel, holding it by the strap.)*

As I headed into town for prayers at the Temple, *(traces his route with one hand)* I was met with one of the gruesome realities of our world — a Roman procession of criminals, on their way to being executed by crucifixion. I stood aside to let them pass, and couldn't help counting. There were three of them that day — *(shows the number and traces their path across the room)* — three poor, bloody excuses for humanity, dragging

46

their cross beams, stumbling under the weight. And as I watched, the middle one fell — collapsed, really — *(gestures)* almost at my feet. The beatings had taken their toll. The soldiers lashed him *(imitates their actions)* and cursed him, *(shakes his head)* but it was no use. He had no more strength, and could not go on with his terrible load.

I was so engrossed in the scene the slap startled me. *(Touches his right shoulder, startled.)* It's what we all fear in this occupied land — the Roman sword — the conscription to a labor of dread. I had been tapped into service to bear the cross for *(gestures to the ground)* this pitiful soul, to the place of his execution — in this case, Calvary. No one dares to refuse. *(Shakes his head and gestures in frustration.)* I had no choice but to take his place, and get it over with as quickly as possible. So there I was, right in the middle of the three criminals, looking for all the world as guilty as they.

*(He drops his satchel strap, lays the crown carefully on it, and stands.)* It was a miserable walk, to say the least! *(Gestures behind.)* Behind us came the Jews, a bunch of wailing women, and the jeering crowds. I was called names I had never even heard before! And the wailers *(he grimaces and covers his ears)* — the women — filling the air with their mournful protests, making the whole sordid affair worse. Calvary could not come too soon, so I could be away on my business. It was a scene I didn't want to witness.

*(He takes a step or two, then turns.)* After a lot of pushing and shoving, stumbling, cursing and shouting, finally we got there. I deposited my load and turned to go. But then something happened — my eyes met the eyes of the man destined for that horrendous cross. They were desperate — yet grateful. And in that moment I could not leave — I had to stay. *(He turns away, remembering, and shakes his head.)* Sadly, everything went as I had feared. The stretching, the binding, the nailing, the drugged wine. Only that middle one — the one I carried for — refused the drugs. The sounds of the onlookers as they gawked and jeered. Again I turned to go, but the scene called me back. Now the other two criminals were shouting and cursing, and I heard one say *(he points to the left of center)*, "Aren't you claiming to be the Messiah? Do something! Save yourself and us!" I thought, "Here you are guilty as sin, man. Why should anyone try to save you?"

*(He points again to the right of center.)* But then the other criminal spoke up. His tone was different — I don't think he was mocking as the first had done. "Lord," he begged in his agony, "I know I deserve this sentence, but — would you remember me when you enter your Kingdom?" The question stopped me in my tracks. Surely he didn't expect Jesus to come down from the cross and set up an earthly kingdom? Maybe he was delirious from the beatings and the drugs, I thought. Or, does he know something I don't know?

I looked up at the middle cross to see if this Jesus had the strength to answer. *(He turns his back to the congregation, and looks slightly upward, as though listening.)* And he did. I heard him clearly. He said, *(turns back to congregation, arms stretched out as on a cross)* "Today you will be with me in paradise." Incredibly, this Jesus seemed to have some connection to the very presence of God! I had been seeking God all my life — seeking assurance of eternal life — keeping the Law and living righteously. And here Jesus was, promising this *(points right)* wreck of humanity — this *(gestures with open hand)* convicted and guilty sinner — this law breaker — instant access to the bliss of God's paradise.

*(Points to someone in the congregation and asks intently.)* Could Jesus actually forgive sins? Sins as terrible as the thieves had been perpetrating? I'm still pondering that question. *(Stooping, he picks up the crown of thorns and studies it.)* Who was this Jesus, anyway? *(Grabbing his satchel, he exits as if continuing his journey, down the platform steps and out the right side of the worship area.)*

**Minister:** *(Snuffs the second candle, the spotlight dims more, and he leads in prayer.)* God who came into this world in your Son Jesus, to seek and save the lost, we stand amazed at the depth and width and height of your forgiveness to sinners. We also know that, like that condemned thief, we deserve the punishment of death. And, like him, we ask for the mercy and grace you offer. If you can forgive him, you can forgive us. And, if you can forgive us, you can forgive anyone who comes in sincere repentance. Cleanse us — sinners all. Make us your children, and bring us one day into your paradise. Under the umbrella of "whosoever will may come," we pray in the name of our Savior, Jesus. Amen.

### Word Three: "Love"
### Jesus' Mother Mary — "Dear woman, here is your son ..."

**Congregational Song:** "Beneath The Cross Of Jesus" (verses 1 and 2)

**Scripture Reading: John 19:23-27**

**Jesus' Mother Mary:** *(Mary and John the Apostle enter together from a platform door, she on his arm. She is elderly and grieving, wearing a dark tunic, with dark veil wrapped around her head and shoulders. John also wears a dark tunic, with dark head square. The spotlight is slightly diminished from the previous actor. Mary steps into the light slowly, and John sits on the bench to listen.)* I made that robe for him myself — with my own hands. It was my last gift to him last year, just before the winter. *(Her shoulders stoop, her head drops, her voice lowers to an angry whisper.)* And they took it! Those godless, Gentile soldiers *(gestures to the ground where they gambled)* gambled for it and took it! *(Her hands turn palms up, empty.)* And now I have nothing. He is gone, and I have nothing to remember him by.

**John:** *(Stepping forward to comfort her, his arm around her.)* I'm here, Aunt Mary. You are not alone.

**Mary:** *(Patting his hand.)* Yes, John, you are here. Thank God you are here. *(Explains to the audience.)* Jesus gave John to me as he was dying. Can you imagine? In his pain and agony, Jesus saw me, and said *(gestures back and forth, whispering hoarsely in her grief)*, "Mother, John is now your son. John, Mary is now your mother." He took care of me, even as he died. *(John hugs her slightly, and sits back down on the bench.)*

But I am not surprised. Family has always been so important to Jesus. Love has always been his way. Even when he was a small boy *(gestures waist height)* he was a good son. And in these last years — such busy years — he found time to come home now and then. *(Turns profile to speak to John.)* Oh, his brothers — they are good boys too, but they do not believe in him — and they had no patience with his wanderings and miracles.

48

*(Turns back to the congregation.)* They would have kept him home in the shop. But Jesus loved them still. He loved us all. But now *(she turns back to John, who stands and receives her)* he is gone. My Jesus is gone. *(John helps her sit on the bench, and sits beside her.)*

**Minister's Prayer:** *(He snuffs out the third candle, and the spotlight dims a little more. Then leads the congregation in prayer.)* God of love, who gave your Son Jesus to the world in love, teach us that the priority of this world must be love. And by the example of our Savior on the cross, may we reach out to those of our own families at this holy season, to see their needs and be quick to help. Help us rise above the pettiness of family rivalries and conflicting interests, and be who we should be. In the name of our loving Savior, we pray. Amen.

**Word Four: "Forsaken"**
**John the Apostle — "My God, my God, why have you forsaken me?"**

**Scripture Reading: Mark 15:33-36**

**John the Apostle:** *(He rises from the bench and steps into the slightly diminished spotlight.)* It was a wrenching day — the worst day of my life. The pain, the blood, the waiting, the fear, the feeling of utter helplessness. *(His hands make fists at his sides.)* My best friend was dying on that sadistic Roman cross, and I could do nothing but stand and watch. I wanted to run, but I stayed. I stayed for Aunt Mary *(gestures to the bench)* and my mother, and the women who were beside themselves with grief. But I also stayed for Jesus — I couldn't leave him to die alone.

*(Shakes his head in sad remembrance.)* God knows we had forsaken him enough that weekend. *(Gestures east to the mountain.)* We forsook him in Gethsemane when he called us to watch and pray for him. *(Gestures the opposite way, to the city.)* We forsook him when the soldiers came, and we all thought they would arrest us along with Jesus. And now — today — look around. *(Gestures a wide arc.)* Where are the crowds that paraded with him into the Jerusalem a week ago? Where are all those he healed, all those he fed, all those he taught and blessed? They, too, have forsaken him. *(Steps down one platform step, keeping a foot on stage level.)*

Of all the things Jesus said from the cross that day, the saddest, for me, was *(turns his face upward toward heaven)* "My God, my God, why have you forsaken me?" Had even the Father turned his face away? Is that why the sky was dark? *(He turns to speak to Mary.)* He said it in the language of his heart, Aunt Mary. The language he used as a little boy. *"Eloi, Eloi, lama sabachthani?"* *(Turns back.)* I don't know if the Father had really left him alone, or if Jesus had just reached the limits of his faith and endurance. To die is terrible enough — but to die feeling alone — *(He turns away, shaking his head in despair. Mary rises, and they exit together the way they came in.)*

**Minister's Prayer:** *(He snuffs the fourth candle, the spotlight diminishes slightly, and he leads the congregation in prayer.)* Our God, who is there in our darkest hours, give us light to understand

49

the burden of our Savior's prayer. We who know the results of our sin, recognize the feeling of separation that comes when we disobey you. We who were born in sin — who are slaves to our sinful natures without your deliverance — we identify with the sense of alienation that burdens us when we transgress against you. But our perfect Lord, who had never known sin, was a stranger to that separation. And when he took on himself our sin, and the consequences of that sin, the rift in his oneness with you surely broke his heart — and yours. Watching, we can only bow in our deepest souls and say, "Thank you, God, for our costly salvation." In the name of our sinless Lord, we pray. Amen.

**Choral or Solo Music:** "Surely, He Hath Borne Our Griefs" from *The Messiah;* or "O Sacred Head, Now Wounded"

## Word Five: "Suffering"
## Mary Magdalene — "I am thirsty"

**Scripture Reading: John 19:28-29 and Hebrews 4:15-16**

**Congregational Song:** "My Jesus, I Love Thee" (verses 1 and 2)

**Mary Magdalene:** *(She enters from the platform, wearing a dark tunic, and a dark veil wound over her head and shoulders. She carries a **water jug** on one shoulder, and sits on the bench to speak.)* Mercifully, his suffering was over and he could rest the rest of death before day's end. Oh, how greatly he suffered! There can be no death worse than the death by crucifixion. *(She sets down the jug and shakes her head sadly at the memory.)*

Jesus was no stranger to suffering, of course. *(Gestures to the east.)* On the road he often had known hunger and thirst. He was often desperately tired, and without a bed, or *(gestures broadly to the sky)* exposed to the storms in an open boat. And — maybe worse than the physical pain — he knew rejection from family and neighbors, ridicule from the leaders, betrayal from close friends.

*(She stands and walks forward slowly, leaving the jug by the bench.)* But this day was different — worse — much worse! Before he reached the cross, he had been beaten nearly to death. He was so weak from loss of blood. *(Reaches for her brow.)* His head must have throbbed from the thorns which so cruelly tore into his brow. By afternoon his thirst was raging, and we wanted so much to help — *(reaches up both hands, as if to lift him)* to take him down — to cool his tongue and salve his awful wounds. *(Her hands fall back to her head.)* But we were helpless against the swords of the soldiers. *(Her hands drop limply.)* We wished for the angels to save him — but none came. *(Holds her face in both hands, shaking her head in frustration.)* We cried. We prayed. We could not stay — we could not leave.

*(She pauses and turns.)* For the longest he did not cry out. He had prayed for his tormentors, and answered the thief. He had comforted his mother, but asked nothing for himself. Finally, in the late afternoon, he asked for a drink. Someone offered him cheap, sour wine; but it was almost over. *(Pauses, shaking her head in hopelessness.)* He was

50

about to die. *(She turns and picks up her jug to go.)* Mercifully, God let him die. *(Mary exits in the way she entered.)*

**Minister's Prayer:** *(He snuffs the fifth candle, the spotlight dims slightly more, and he leads the congregation in prayer.)* Jesus, our High Priest before the Father, how we grieve at your unbearable suffering for us that day. But how we thank God that you understand the pain and burdens of our lives, and can intercede for us today. Thank you that you showed us how to endure the fatigue and fear, the grief and suffering, that life brings our way. We call on you to make us strong in you today. In the name of our Savior and Friend, we pray. Amen.

**Word Six: "Victory!"**
**Pilate, the Governor — "It is finished!"**

**Scripture Reading: John 19:30 and Romans 5:6-8**

**Pilate, the Governor:** *(His costume is a white tunic hemmed in red braid. Over his shoulder is draped a white stole, also bordered in red. He wears sandals, and his head is uncovered. Pilate enters from the back and strides down the main aisle, speaking. The Centurion follows two paces behind, walking stiffly, hand on his short sword.)* They tell me it is over! This Jesus is finally dead! Why, I ask you *(gestures to either side)* did this nightmare have to occur on my watch? And why now?

*(He mounts the platform steps with his guard close behind. The Centurion moves to the side and stands at attention, while Pilate steps to stage center, still speaking.)* As if I haven't had enough trouble with these *(points in a broad sweep outside the room)* cantankerous Jews of late! Now they bring me an innocent man, and threaten me with disloyalty to Caesar if I do not have him killed. What am I to choose? My job or my honor? *(Sarcastically, turning.)* Well, as I told my wife, honor does not pay well, from what I hear.

*(He paces briskly, glaring at the audience.)* Well, it's finished now. Whatever purpose it served for the Jews, it surely saved my neck. *(Turning to the Centurion, gesturing and barking orders rudely.)* Take him down! Get rid of the body! And put a guard on the tomb! I want to hear no more of this Galilean "King." *(The Centurion bows. Pilate exits the nearest door, with the Centurion close behind.)*

**Minister's Prayer:** *(He snuffs the sixth candle, the spotlight dims to almost dark, and he leads the congregation in prayer.)* Merciful God, your great plan of history was fulfilled in that single cry, "It is finished!" To the world it is foolishness, but to us who are being saved, it is the power by which we become the children of God. We know that it is through the blood of Jesus Christ, our sacrificial lamb, that we can be forgiven of our sins and be put right with you again. Today we ask anew for that wonderful grace that is greater than all the combined sins of humankind. In the name of our crucified Lord, we ask. Amen.

**Congregational Song:** "Grace Greater Than Our Sin"

# Word Seven: "Hope"
## Joseph of Arimathea — "Father, into your hands I commit my spirit"

**Scripture Reading: Luke 23:46-54**

**Joseph of Arimathea:** *(He enters from the right, walking slowly. Over his dark tunic he wears a **white prayer shawl**, and he carries **a large, heavy box or urn**, such as would hold ancient burial spices. Reaching the stage area he pauses, looking over the congregation silently a moment, then speaks gently.)* You are his friends, and I know you will be relieved to know that we took him down from the cross and laid him in my new tomb to rest. It was a gentle ending to a violent and tragic day.

*(Speaking to the congregation on his left.)* I was not there for the entire day. The trial sickened me, and, I must admit, I had no stomach for *(gestures up as to the cross)* watching such a good man suffer and die. I was a believer, you see, *(hand to chest)* but secretly; so I struggled all day with what I knew was right. Late in day I came, and stood with his friends and family a short distance from the cross. Jesus had already been declared dead. Nicodemus also came, and we two then went to Pilate to claim the body. *(He nods, as though anticipating the next question.)* Yes, *(crosses his forehead)* we marked ourselves as his followers by so doing. But — it was time — perhaps beyond time.

*(Speaking now to his right.)* It was a senseless death, you know — at least from man's point of view. Jesus was an innocent man, and had committed no sin — *(shakes his head and wags his index finger back and forth)* surely none worthy of death — surely none that merited a criminal's death. It was all an act of jealous rage and fear. The Council feared his popularity and his radical ideas about people and worship. *(Confidentially.)* And — most of all — the loss of their precious authority, their status, their jobs.

*(Paces slowly to the left.)* But now Jesus is at rest. We buried him well. *(He turns back to the congregation with a smile.)* Did you hear his last words? "Father, into your hands I commit my spirit." Beautiful words. Hopeful words. I believe that is just what has happened — *(lifts his hands toward heaven)* his spirit has returned to the God who sent him here to us. He promised us that, you know. He said, "I go to prepare a place for you." Jesus was always a man of his word. *(Nods confidently.)* We will be with him again in another world — a place free of pain and contention and threats. A place where his *(gestures broadly as to the world)* Kingdom of love and kindness can grow unhindered. We can all take great hope in that. *(He exits to the left, leaving the lighted Christ Candle on the table.)*

**Minister's Closing:** *(With only a dim spotlight remaining, he picks up the lighted Christ Candle and holds it as he speaks.)* We leave this final candle burning. It is the "Christ Candle," and it symbolizes our hope for eternity. Our Savior is not dead, but alive. The candle may have been hidden from view for a while, but his Light remains, and he will return for each of us in his time. For this he came — to show us the way to God. In this we hope — that we will be with him again in Eternity one day.

**Congregational Song:** "Because He Lives" (verses 1 and 3)

**Benediction Prayer:** Now, our Father, dismiss us in peace as we go to contemplate this most important event of humankind's long history: the atoning death of your only begotten Son. His work is finished. Our salvation has been purchased. And we have the certain hope of Eternity with him one day. In the name of our glorified Savior, we pray. Amen. *(The congregation exits to quiet music.)*

# Chapter 6
# Surprise At Sunrise
# An Early Easter Worship With Children's Drama

**Description:** Worshipers gather at first dawn light on Easter morning to re-live the joy. Four vignettes, with child actors, depict the resurrection discovery in pantomime, scripture, and songs of praise. Also included are an Easter meditation and a surprise "Jesus and the Children" climax. Recommended as an outdoor sunrise service.

**Preparations:** Enlist three teams to prepare for this service: a **Drama Team** to produce the children's drama vignettes; a **Worship Team**, to plan the music and meditation portions; and an **Arrangements Team** to set up the chairs, stage, and worship furnishings. Begin planning at least one month before Easter (much farther ahead if an outdoor facility must be secured).

**1. Drama Team:** Carefully read the five vignettes, four depicting the resurrection surprises, and a fifth of Jesus and the Children. Enlist a **drama coach** to cast **children, ages 8 to 12**, in all the roles except the **Jesus person.** Children's **costumes** will be needed, and mothers will want time and instruction about making these. (See, "Costumes" below.) **Several rehearsals** and some Bible study will be needed by the children. Since the children do not have speaking parts, sound amplification will not be needed by this group. If the program is outdoors, use the natural dawn light without spotlighting.

**Characters Needed** *(Child Actors:)* Mary Magdalene, The Other Mary, Salome, Peter, and John; *(Adult Actor:)* Jesus. Also child "extras."

**Costumes:** Bible people wore very drab colors and worn fabrics, with no ironing. Ask mothers to make the children's long tunics from dull tones of gray, blue, or tan. (Child-size patterns are available in fabric stores.) Boys will need corresponding, 24-inch head squares of muted stripes or solids, tied with a narrow headband. Girls will need veils of muted light colors, in lengths 4 feet by 2 feet. Children should wear sandals. If the weather is cool, they may wear warmer clothing hidden under their tunics. Note the few **simple props** required and prepare these also.

The **Jesus player's costume** is a simple white robe, and he should have a short beard, wear sandals, and be bare-headed. Consult Bible illustrations and recent videos depicting Jesus for resurrection costume ideas.

**Children's Rehearsals:** Children will better understand their roles if a simple **Bible study** is done at the beginning of each rehearsal. (It might be possible to include these studies and rehearsals in the children's regular Sunday school hour during the month before Easter.) Invite one of the **children's teachers** to lead the two studies. At the first rehearsal, have children read and talk about Mark 16:1-8, and practice acting the first two vignettes. **Send them home with instructions, so that parents can help them** work on parts for the first two vignettes between rehearsals. At the second rehearsal, let them read and talk about John 20:1-16, and work on parts for the third and fourth vignettes. Again inform parents how to help them play out the last two vignettes at home.

A third, **dress rehearsal will be needed, preferably in the location** where the worship service will be held, so children can fit their actions and conversation to the setting. At the final rehearsal, the **person who will read scriptures** during the presentation should be present to work with the children. Also at this last rehearsal, **explain the fifth vignette** to the children, so they will understand that the actor playing Jesus is not the real Jesus, but that they may treat him joyfully as though he were. Ask them, "How would you have felt if you had been there on that first Easter morning when Jesus came back to life from the grave?"

**Notes about children and drama:** When working with children, expect them to be playful, but help them balance that with discussion of the importance and seriousness of the Easter event. Give much praise, fuss very little, and enjoy their joyful spirits. Much of the value of this drama experience will be their becoming more impressed with the events of Easter. The production itself will be secondary. Several children may play out each role before final cast selection is made. There are **several "extras"** in the final scene with Jesus, so every child who wishes to be in the drama may have a part. On Easter morning, when the drama is presented, children should arrive 15 minutes early in costume. **A children's worker** will need to be at each of the right and left backstage locations with a script, to receive the children and help them hear and follow their cues.

2. **Worship Team:** Ministers and musicians will want to talk through and plan the adult portion of the service, which includes scripture readings, hymns, and a resurrection meditation. Determine whether a minister or a children's worker will do the four scripture readings. Also, this team will see to the **stage furnishings** (pulpit stand, chairs, musical equipment, sound amplification) and **printed worship program** with notes about the drama cast. **Flowers** for worshipers to place at the cross will need to be purchased and stored in containers of water for freshness. **A choir** is optional, but consider using a teenage choir if one is available. If **refreshments or breakfast** are to follow, the Worship Team will enlist persons to handle that.

3. **Arrangements Team:** Particularly if the service is outdoors, **chairs for worshipers** may be needed, because the actors will need to come through aisles as they act; and it is difficult for older attenders to sit on blankets on the ground. Set the service up as a worship event, with a simple **stage area** for ministers and musicians. (This does not need to be elevated above the level of worshipers, but may be ground level.) Actors will need a way by which they may "appear" during a vignette, and "disappear" on the opposite side of the stage area. If held outdoors, actors could appear and disappear from behind a building or grove of trees. If there is no natural barrier, a simple **partition or screen** will need to be placed at both ends of the stage area. (These could be room dividers or wide trellises of vines and flowers.)

A wonderful, traditional focal point can be made by having a carpenter construct **three wooden crosses,** (at least six feet tall) and secure them in the ground several feet behind or to the side of the stage area. A mound of fresh dirt with a few large stones can cover the bases. (Worshipers will put fresh flowers here as the service begins.)

---

**The Service At A Glance:**

**Quiet Music**
**Placing Flowers At The Cross**
**Congregational Song**
**Readings And Vignettes**
**Congregational Song**
**Minister's Meditation**
**Solo Or Congregational Song**
**Closing Vignette**
**Benediction Praise Chorus**

---

**Quiet Music:** "In The Garden" or taped instrumental Easter music

**Placing Flowers At The Cross:** As worshipers arrive, let youth ushers help each one select a cut flower from large pitchers or buckets of blooms. (Any mix of individual carnations, daffodils, tulips, chrysanthemums, or lilies would be good choices.) As quiet music plays, invite everyone to go to the crosses before being seated, and lay his or her flower at the foot of the center cross as an act of devotion. If printed programs are being used, place these ahead of time on worshiper's chairs.

**Congregational Song:** "When I Survey The Wondrous Cross" (all verses)

**First Reading: Mark 16:1-3**

**First Vignette:** As the verses are being read, children portraying Mary Magdalene, the other Mary, and Salome appear from behind the barrier at stage left. Each carries a decorative box or urn of "spices" with which to anoint Jesus' body. They walk in a close huddle, asking (silently or in whispers) "What shall we do about that heavy stone?" "Who will be there to help us move it?" "Dare we break the seal of Pilate to put spices on Jesus' body?" "I don't understand why they had to kill him." Because they are pantomiming the scripture verses and not speaking aloud, hand gestures and facial expressions will be very important. After walking across the front of the stage area, they disappear behind the barrier to stage right.

**Second Reading: Mark 16:4-8**

**Second Vignette:** As verses 7 and 8 are read, the same three girl actors reappear from stage right, running back to the place from which they originally came at stage left. In their arms they still carry the vessels of spices, holding them tightly as they run. Their faces are frightened. Mary Magdalene is running faster, with the other two trailing about half a stage behind. As Mary Magdalene disappears at stage left, the other two slow down, whispering to each other, "Where could his body be?" "Do you think someone has stolen it?" They also then disappear to stage left.

**Third Reading: John 20:1-9**

**Third Vignette:** As the verses are being read, Mary Magdalene, Peter, and John appear from stage left, talking with animation. She is pantomiming, "No, his body is gone — it is missing! We could not find him in the tomb." Peter and John are looking at her, and then at each other, shaking their heads in disbelief saying, "That can't possibly be! Surely you are mistaken." Then Peter begins to run across the stage area toward stage right, and John comes after him but runs faster, passing Peter on the way. John, and then Peter, disappear at stage right. Mary Magdalene also follows with her box of spices, but more slowly. She stands at stage right, but does not disappear behind the barrier.

**Fourth Reading: John 20:10-16**

**Fourth Vignette:** As these verses are read, Peter and John re-appear and stop to visit with Mary Magdalene at stage right. Peter is holding a folded white napkin (about two feet square) taken from the tomb. They are shaking their heads and whispering, "He really is gone! We have no idea where they have taken his body." She is saying, "That's what I told you. The tomb was empty when we came earlier." John says, "Well, I guess all we can do right now is go back to the upper room and wait." Peter hands Mary the folded napkin, and he and John walk slowly to stage left and disappear, while Mary Magdalene stays at stage right. She presses the napkin to her face, as though grieving. Suddenly she turns around, as though seeing the Lord, and falls to her knees in worship. During the singing of the next hymn, she stands and runs back to stage left, dropping the napkin as she runs. She disappears upon reaching stage left, ending these first four vignettes.

**Congregational Song:** "Christ The Lord Is Risen Today, Alleluia!" (all verses)
(*During the last verse of the song all the children — those who have been playing the roles, and other "extras" who wish to be in the drama — take seats which have been reserved for them at the front of the congregation.*)

**Minister's Meditation:** It would be appropriate here for the minister to bring a brief message on some truth about the risen Christ.

**Solo:** "In The Garden" (or Congregational Song, "He Lives!")

**Fifth Vignette:** As this song begins, a young man dressed to look like Jesus starts down the center aisle from the back, stopping at several rows to greet worshipers with an embrace, a pat on the shoulder, a smile, and a hug. When he is more than half way to the front, workers cue the children to run happily to him, to hug him and be blessed by him, and he touches them all. As the song finishes, the Jesus player disappears at stage right, and the children return to their seats or to their parents.

**Benediction Praise Chorus:** "He Is Lord!"

(*Consider following this worship time with refreshments of hot chocolate and coffee, or a light breakfast served nearby.*)

# Chapter 7
# The Week Of Weeks
# Seven Interactive Readings For Pentecost

**Description:** For each of the seven Sundays between Easter and Pentecost, find here a scripture reading with interaction from one or two of the Bible personalities within it. The actors respond from within the congregation in memorized dialogue with the minister or lay reader. Actors may be costumed or in contemporary dress. The ten-minute readings are designed to be integrated into post-Easter season worship services. For continuity through the fifty days, two Pentecost worship banners are suggested.

**Preparations Needed:** A **drama coach** is needed to enlist the actors, make arrangements, and direct the rehearsal for each interactive reading. He or she may enlist help to prepare costumes and simple props, and arrange for sound as needed. In addition, enlist a **banner-maker** to make banners or lead a banner workshop. (See plans below.)

**Characters Needed:**

*First Sunday After Easter:* Cleopas, The Walk to Emmaus
*Second Sunday After Easter:* Thomas and John, Realization in the Upper Room
*Third Sunday After Easter:* James, His Brother's Keeper
*Fourth Sunday After Easter:* John and Peter, Breakfast on the Shore
*Fifth Sunday After Easter:* Matthew, The Commissioning and Ascension
*Sixth Sunday After Easter:* His Mother Mary and Salome, Praying with Joy
*Pentecost Sunday:* Peter, The Power Comes

**Readers:** The scripture passages each week may be read by either a minister or a lay reader, but will require one rehearsal of the Reader with the actor(s) for effective presentation. (See the following section.) Consider a woman Reader, for voice contrast with the actors who will be mostly men. Whereas the actors will need to memorize their parts, the Reader may become familiar with the script, and speak from it.

**Casting, Costuming, and Rehearsals:** Selecting actors who can accurately express the personalities of the Bible persons is important. Read through each part, noting church members or others who seem suited. Note that two actors appear twice: John comes on weeks 2 and 4, and Peter on 4 and 7.

As noted, actors may be dressed in biblical garments, or in contemporary church clothing. The plan is that they be seated within the congregation, and not designated in the printed worship program, so that their rising to dialogue with the Reader is a surprise to most worshipers. If biblical dress is chosen, each will need a rather plain tunic, with head square or veil, bare feet with sandals, and **small carry-on props**, as suggested in each part. If the decision is for contemporary dress, still use the carry-ons as indicated.

Actors will need to be enlisted and given parts at least two weeks before their date of performance. Ask that they memorize their parts before the rehearsal, practicing alone with attention to voice emphasis and gestures. When they rehearse with the designated Reader, coach them further on gestures and voice, so that the dialogues have a feeling of spontaneity and reality. Work through each script several times, until both Reader and actor begin to feel very comfortable. If the worship area is large, lapel microphones will be needed on the actors. In this case, include sound technicians in the rehearsals.

**Preparing Pentecost Banners:** To bring continuity to the post-Easter season, two large worship banners are suggested. If there is no experienced banner-maker in the congregation, consider scheduling **a banner workshop** the month before Easter. Invite persons with artistic or fabric skills to help design and make the two banners. Banners can be made most simply on a felt background, with felt letters and artwork attached with fabric glue or bonding. Other **easy mediums** include taffeta, lamé, or satin, with artwork attached by a bonding fabric. (By this method, fabrics must be able to withstand the heat of an iron. Applique is another option.) Fabric paints and trims around the artwork, and fringe along the lower edge, dress banners up.

Most often banners are fastened to a decorative drapery rod by several loops which are sewn into the top hem. A finished size of at least 30 inches wide by 45 inches high is recommended — larger for a large worship room. If possible, hang the completed banners on the walls at both sides of the platform area on the first Sunday following Easter, and leave them for the seven-Sunday event.

*Banner Making:* Banner makers will need to cut exact patterns for words and artwork from paper, and determine exact placement on the banner background, before beginning to cut or bond the materials. If a commercial banner pattern is not used, artwork can be enlarged from Christian clip art; and lettering stencils are available in educational supply stores. Keep in mind that simpler patterns are more easily understood by worshipers, while complicated patterns may obscure the meanings. Lettering should be at least five inches tall. Designs are suggested here as a beginning place, or you may find appropriate ones in banner-making books at a Christian bookstore.

**As a theme** for these two Pentecost banners, use Acts 1:8. Caption the first banner, *"Receive the Power,"* and the second, *"Be My Witness."* Select a rich red or purple background fabric.

*Banner One: "Receive the Power"* — To bridge from Easter to Pentecost, use an empty cross on the first banner, swagged with a bright drape and a crown of thorns. Place the cross to the left center of the banner. Overlay gold caption wording across the lower part of the cross. Place letters about eight inches above the bottom hem. Emphasize the word *POWER* by capitalizing it and making it slightly larger than the first two words.

*Banner Two: "Be My Witness"* — Overlay a white dove onto a tall gold flame (or several smaller flames closely placed) and affix these to the right center of the banner. Balance this artwork with the size of the cross used on the first banner, so they look like a pair. Place the gold caption wording (to match the style used on Banner One) on the lower portion, emphasizing the word *WITNESS* by the same method used on the first banner. Overlap part of the caption onto the flame symbols, and set letters the same distance above the bottom hem as was done on the first banner.

### First Sunday After Easter
### Cleopas: The Walk To Emmaus
### Luke 24:13-45

*(Cleopas is seated in the congregation, wearing a dull-colored tunic and simple head square, topped by a black turban. In his hand is **a small scroll**, which may also be used as a prompt for his speaking parts. As the Reader begins, Cleopas opens his scroll, but remains seated.)*

**Reader: Luke 24:13-16**

**Cleopas:** *(Raising his hand slightly and interrupting rather loudly, but remaining seated.)* It was the sunset — partly.

**Reader:** *(Looking for the voice; then speaking to Cleopas)* Excuse me?

**Cleopas:** *(Standing tentatively and pointing to the west.)* It was the sunset — the sun was in our eyes as we walked west into the sunset, and we couldn't see him well. *(Slight pause.)* And we weren't expecting to see him. *(Pause.)* He was dead, you know. *(Sits down.)*

**Reader:** *(Unsure of how to respond.)* Um ... yes, we see. Thank you. *(Continues the scripture where he left off at the interruption.)* **Luke 24:16-21.**

**Cleopas:** *(Standing and waving slightly to be heard.)* We *had* hoped that, you know. Hoped it with all our hearts.

**Reader:** *(With patience, pausing his reading.)* I'm sure you did, Friend.

**Cleopas:** And now ... now we felt so hopeless ... so broken. *(Shakes his head sadly.)* Nothing was making sense in our lives. We had put all our plans and our futures into this Jesus, and *(pausing for words, empty-handed)* now he was gone. And it was even worse because the women — Mary and the others — they were so crazy with grief they kept telling us they had seen his ghost. *(Gestures into the air futilely.)* They imagined angels, and even thought

61

he might have come back from the dead. *(Shakes his head in confusion, and slowly takes his seat again.)*

**Reader:** *(With sympathy.)* I'm sure it was very hard to know what to believe. I'll continue the story. **Luke 24:22-26.**

**Cleopas:** *(Standing again, now excited.)* That's when it all began to make sense to us! Pardon me for interrupting again, but that is when we began to see things more plainly — when he explained it all so clearly. *(Snaps his fingers toward the sky.)* It was like a light dawned on us.

**Reader:** *(Motioning permission.)* Tell us, Sir — I'm sorry I didn't get your name —

**Cleopas:** I apologize, Brother. I'm Cleopas. I'm one who was on the road that day.

**Reader:** Brother Cleopas, tell us, Sir — what did Jesus say to you when he explained the scriptures?

**Cleopas:** Oh, *(shakes his head)* so many things. He explained all the old stories, *(gestures behind him)* clear back to Moses, and made it all fit together — like a broken plate, *(makes a dish-sized circle with his hands)* with all the pieces glued back like new.

**Reader:** *(To Cleopas.)* Shall I go on with the story?

**Cleopas:** *(Nods, takes his seat.)*

**Reader:** **Luke 24:26-31.** *(Stops here to ask Cleopas.)* Is that when you realized who he was, Cleopas?

**Cleopas:** *(Remaining seated, smiling.)* Yes, at the table! When he broke the bread, we knew him — and then *(snaps his fingers)* he was gone! We just sat there, stunned, trying to understand what we had just experienced. But our hearts were warm within us from those few minutes with the Savior.

**Reader:** It must have been a wonderful kind of stunned. Now, it says here *(continuing to read)* **Luke 24:32-33.** *(Interrupting himself.)* Cleopas, how far was it back to town?

**Cleopas:** Pretty far, Friend. About seven miles. And it was getting dark.

**Reader:** That's pretty far. *(Continues reading.)* **Luke 24:33-36.**

**Cleopas:** *(Standing, excited.)* Now you're getting to the good part. He was there! *(Pointing toward the front of the room.)* Jesus was standing right there in the middle of us. And everyone saw it, so nobody could say we were having hallucinations or something. It scared us half to death, but he was right there. *(To the reader.)* Is that all there in your story?

**Reader:** I believe so. Right here. *(Continues, as Cleopas sits down.)* **Luke 24:36-43.**

**Cleopas:** *(Standing.)* That's correct — that's just how it happened. He took food, and they knew he wasn't a ghost. And by then everyone was so happy they just about raptured right out of the room. Oh, *(turns around to face the congregation behind him, clasping his hand to his heart)* it was the happiest night of my life. My Jesus was alive, and I knew it beyond any shadow of doubt! My hopes were revived — *(both palms upward, excited)* I could believe again. Jesus was the Messiah from God, sent to take away our sins, just as he had said. And my broken world was *(makes the dish sized circle again)* all glued back together. *(He sits back down.)*

**Reader:** *(Addressing Cleopas.)* Well, that was quite a story, Friend. And now, thanks to you, we can all feel as though we were there. Thank you for coming to worship with us today.

**Congregational Song:** "He Lives!"

<br>

## Second Sunday After Easter
## Thomas And John: Realization In The Upper Room
## John 20:19-29

*(Thomas, who will be the main speaker, sits in the midst of the congregation. John, who is a supporting actor, sits to one side and farther back. Both wear simple tunics, with head squares. Thomas' square is topped with a wide sash, while John's is tied back, bandana style.)*

**Reader:** This morning we will read of two occasions when Jesus appeared to his disciples in the upper room following his resurrection. This first one happened the evening of the very day he was resurrected, and the second one week later. **John 20:19-20.**

**John:** *(Standing and interrupting gently.)* You have no idea, Sir, how happy we were at that moment — how good it was to see him alive again — to hear him say, "Peace," to us.

**Reader:** *(Searching for the voice.)* After all you had been through, watching him beaten and crucified, watching him die — you are right, we really cannot imagine what this moment meant to all of you.

**John:** *(Motioning for the Reader to proceed.)* Please read on, Sir. These words are so very important to all of us here. *(He is seated.)*

**Reader: John 20:21-23.**

**John:** *(Standing reverently, motioning to speak.)* Sir, I wonder if we heard those three very important things Jesus said to us. They were spoken so quickly, but they turned the world upside down.

**Reader:** *(Looking back at his text.)* Three things? Let's see — well, he said, "Peace be with you," a second time.

**John:** We were in terror, Sir. Hiding, fearing the worst, wondering if they would come after us next. I guess that is why he said, "Peace," twice — to calm us, so we could hear what he was going to tell us next.

**Reader:** *(Again searching and pointing to the text.)* Next he said, "As the Father has sent me, I am sending you." What did he mean by that, John?

**John:** He was reminding us of our mission. We had forgotten, in all the terrible events of the weekend, why he had called us, and what we had been trained to do. And without him, we didn't know where to begin. He was focusing our minds — giving us direction again.

**Reader:** *(Once again searching the text.)* And there was a third thing here?

**John:** Yes, Sir. Then he breathed his Spirit into us — his very own life and power — so we could continue his work in the world. *(Turns around to the congregation.)* Can you realize how very important that moment was to us all — how it changed our lives? *(Spying Thomas sitting across the room.)* Ah, Thomas! And you almost missed the whole thing!

**Thomas:** *(Remaining seated, nodding, somewhat embarrassed.)*

**Reader:** *(Looking back and forth to the two.)* Should I read on, Brothers? *(They nod, and Reader continues.)* **John 20:24-25.**

**Thomas:** *(Standing and interrupting.)* Sir, please let me explain. *(Turns around to the congregation.)* I know I sounded skeptical, but all they were telling me — well — it just sounded too simple — too good to be true. We had all been just crushed by the crucifixion of our Lord. I just had to have some proof before I could allow myself to hope again.

**Reader:** *(Smiling and sympathetic.)* That makes sense to me, Thomas. Shall I read on? *(Thomas nods and sits down, and Reader continues.)* **John 20:26-27.** *(He stops to address Thomas again.)* How did you feel at that point, Friend?

**Thomas:** *(Standing, turning to the congregation, shaking his head thoughtfully.)* I can't really put into words how I felt. I just remember thinking, "He understands! Jesus understands how hard this has been, and how broken I am. He's come to help me work through this." And I was overcome with his love.

**Reader:** And what did you say?

**Thomas:** "My Lord and my God!" *(Very earnestly, addressing the Reader.)* I just fell at his feet and cried, "My Lord and my God!"

**Reader:** And what did Jesus say to you, Thomas?

**Thomas:** He put it all into perspective, as always. I think he said, "Because you have seen and touched me, you have believed; but blessed will be those who have not seen and yet have believed." You see, Sir, my faith was easy — I could reach out *(pantomimes)* and touch those

64

crucified hands. *(Turns to the congregation again.)* And none of you can do that. You must just read about it, and take the leap of faith. That is much harder.

**Reader:** True, my Friend; but Jesus said, we would be blessed if we could believe. We here are all trying to do just that.

**Thomas:** *(Gesturing to the congregation.)* Then say it with me, and receive the blessing. *(Beckons for a unison response.)* Say it with me now: "My Lord and my God!" Say it again: "My Lord and my God!" *(Nods and smiles.)* That's just who he is, people — he is your Lord and your God. And you are truly blessed. *(Thomas is seated.)*

**Congregational Song:** "Majesty" or "O For A Thousand Tongues To Sing"

## Third Sunday After Easter
## James: His Brother's Keeper
## John 7:2-5; 1 Corinthians 15:3-7; Acts 1:12-14

*(James enters the platform just before the scripture reading and takes a chair beside the ministers. If in Bible costume, he wears a tunic of muted stripes, with a light-colored head square, topped by a dark turban. Complete the dress with sash and sandals. He carries a small scroll, wrapped in tapestry and tied with a gold cord. In the scroll is printed 1 Corinthians 15:3-7, which he will later read.)*

**Reader:** *(Not acknowledging James yet.)* This morning we will look into one of the fascinating mysteries of Jesus' post-resurrection appearances during the fifty days from Passover to Pentecost — also called the "Week of Weeks" — seven weeks of seven days. That mystery has to do with the conversion of Jesus' brothers: James, Joseph, Simon, and Judas, as named for us by the Apostle Matthew. Throughout Jesus' ministry years, the brothers did not accept him as God's Messiah, but at the prayer service before Pentecost, Luke tells us they were present. Let me read that exciting truth: **Acts 1:12-14.**

*(Repeating.)* "With his brothers." So the question captivates us: "When did Jesus' brothers believe in him?"

**James:** *(Standing and walking towards the Reader.)* I'm glad you asked, Brother. That question is more important to me than it could ever be to all of you.

**Reader:** *(To the congregation.)* Let me introduce to you our special guest pastor. Meet James, the brother of our Lord, and formerly pastor of the believers in Jerusalem. *(Leads members to applaud politely for their guest, and James acknowledges with a nod of his head.)*

**James:** Sir, you are right in saying my brothers and I had difficulty believing in Jesus. Somehow we just could not *(gestures with both hands, as trying to reach around a post)* get our minds around the idea that our older brother was different than we were — somehow more special to God. We were embarrassed by him — by his showy deeds of healing and teaching — *(gestures to the north)* like that day in Nazareth when he criticized the home folks in the synagogue, and almost got himself thrown down a cliff. We wanted to hide, we were so humiliated.

**Reader:** I have read about that. But I didn't think of how it felt from the family's point of view.

**James:** *(Nods and continues.)* And some of it was jealousy. Our dear mother favored him so, and even took off and traveled *(gestures widely as though traveling)* with him around Galilee and to Jerusalem. Oh — *(shakes his head for emphasis)* she believed in him — she made up for us all. And I guess we resented it. It must have broken her heart that her sons could not get along. Young people can be so hard-headed.

**Reader:** John tells us one of the stories in his Gospel of Jesus. Do you mind if I read that? *(He looks to James for permission, and James nods. He reads, and James stands beside him, head bowed, listening intently.)* **John 7:2-3.**

**James:** *(Leans into the microphone, interrupting.)* We were a little sarcastic there. Almost taunting him, as I recall. We wanted him to play his hand, so to speak. To clear the matter up once and for all.

**Reader:** *(Continuing.)* **John 7:4-5.**

**James:** It all seems rather childish to me now. But at that time we were all tangled up in our doubts. We wanted some proof. Not that all the miracles he had been doing weren't proof enough.

**Reader:** *(Looking puzzled at James.)* So, Brother James, when did it all change? When did you believe?

**James:** Well, it's here *(holds up his scroll)* in Paul's letter to the Corinthians. Here — let me read it for you. *(He unwraps his scroll and reads.)* **1 Corinthians 15:3-4.** *(He stops, points to the words he has just read, and speaks with emphasis.)* I believe that now. I believe that my brother was sent by God to die for our sins, and that he was raised from the dead on the third day — because I have seen him with my own eyes. *(Continues.)* **1 Corinthians 15:5-7.** *(Stops reading, re-rolls his scroll.)* He came to me — and he loved me — and I had to believe.

**Reader:** *(Placing an arm around James and shaking his hand warmly.)* That is quite a testimony, Brother James. What a story! Jesus must have seen great potential in you, to have singled you out for a meeting after he was raised from the dead.

*(Turning to the congregation.)* And James went on to make up for those years of unbelief. He became a great leader among the Jerusalem believers, and even wrote a book to the scattered, persecuted Jewish Christians, which we know as the letter of James, found in our New Testament.

**James:** *(Responding to the Reader.)* But that is no credit to me, Friend. It speaks only of the gracious forgiveness of my brother, the Lord Jesus, whom I love and serve with all my heart. In this way I am somewhat like the Apostle Paul — I can never serve him enough to make up for the years of unbelief and hardship I caused him. I serve out of love, and out of gratitude.

**Reader:** *(Responding to James.)* Faith comes a little harder for some of us. But usually, once our doubts are settled, we are strong in our commitments.

**James:** *(Nods assent.)* It took a while, but now I serve Jesus with all my heart. *(James exits as the song begins.)*

**Congregational Song:** "I Will Sing The Wondrous Story"


## Fourth Sunday After Easter
## John And Peter: Breakfast On The Shore
## John 21:1-24

*(While both John and Peter are guests, initially only John is in the room, with Peter entering later. This should be the same actor who portrayed John when he came with Thomas two weeks ago. If in Bible attire, John wears a long tunic of rough domestic material, with dark leather belt, and sandals. His head square is tied back, bandana style. John is seated with the congregation, on a side aisle and near the front.)*

**Reader:** Our Pentecost scripture today is from John 21, the story of Jesus meeting a group of the disciples on the shore of Galilee, sometime between the resurrection and the ascension. This is a story told only in the Gospel of John. We know that John, whose book was the last of the four to be written, made a point of including in his book many of the stories which were omitted from the other Gospels.

*(He begins to read.)* **John 21:1-3.** *(Then stops to ask the congregation.)* Why do you think these seven men left the ministry for which Jesus had trained them, and went back to the shore?

**John:** *(Standing at his chair, signaling to speak.)* Sir, let me try to answer that, if I may. This was in those forty days *(holds his hands parallel but apart, as if measuring)* between our Lord's resurrection, and when he ascended back to his Father. All of us were from Galilee *(indicates north)* in the general area of the lake, and we had gone home to await further instruction from the Master. In fact, the Lord had commanded us to go home at that time. As for the fishing — well — *(laughs a little)* you heard who suggested that! Peter was antsy that night, and just felt comfortable doing what he knew to do well. Most of us were fishermen by trade, so it was natural to jump on board and go along. We usually followed his lead. *(He sits back down.)*

**Reader:** Thank you, Sir. And may we know your name?

**John:** *(Seated.)* I'm John, Sir — the author of the book from which you read.

**Reader:** *(Surprised and delighted.)* And it is an honor to have you, John. *(Leads the congregation to applaud politely.)* Your insights are helpful to us. Shall I continue the story? *(He receives John's nod, and continues.)* **John 21:4-6.**

**Peter:** *(Enters from the side opposite from John during this reading. If in Bible costume, he wears a short, calf-length, rough and wrinkled tunic, with a rope belt. A **fishing throw net**, such as a seine or cast net, is draped over one shoulder, and he is bare-headed and bare-footed, and a bit disheveled. He stands listening to the Reader, then begins to slowly walk toward the front of the room as he interrupts.)* I remember that night well, Friend. Where did you learn about it?

**Reader:** *(Looking carefully at Peter as he walks forward.)* Don't tell me — you must be the one and only Peter of whom we speak.

**Peter:** *(Nodding and smiling.)* That, Sir, I am.

**Reader:** Well, I read from the book written by your good friend John. *(He points to John, who stands, and walks around to the front to great Peter. They embrace, slap backs, shake hands, and generally act delighted to see each other.)*

**Peter:** *(Speaking to the Reader.)* Sorry to be late. We caught a school and just hated to leave before getting them in.

**John:** *(To Peter.)* How did it go?

**Peter:** Not bad — but not as good as the story he *(points to Reader)* just told. What a night that was! I remember being worn out and discouraged as the dawn broke that day, coming in empty from a night of rowing and tossing nets. *(He fingers the net on his shoulder.)* Fishing is hard work, you know — at least the way we do it on Galilee it is. I was so excited about all those fish, it never even occurred to me to ask, "Who's that guy on shore who helped us out?"

**Reader:** According to the story, it was John who thought about that. Let me read it. *(John and Peter stand listening as he begins reading, but they interrupt.)* **John 21:7-**

**Peter:** Hey! He loved me, too!

**John:** *(Defensively, and a little playfully.)* Sure he did — but *I* wrote the book, and it wouldn't have been polite to use my own name. I had to designate myself some way. *(To the Reader.)* Sorry, Friend. You may read on. It's a good book!

**Reader:** *(Beginning over.)* **John 21:7-8.** *(During the reading John slaps Peter playfully.)*

**John:** *(To Peter.)* Well — that sounds familiar. You jump out of the boat and leave me with all the fish to count, and the nets to clean.

**Peter:** But, John, it was the Lord! It was the Lord! *(Stretches out an arm as toward the shore.)* I had to go to him!

**John:** *(Grasping Peter's upper arm warmly.)* It's okay, Buddy. I like your style. I'd have jumped in, too, but somebody had to hang on to those fish! We needed the money!

**Reader:** So, tell us the rest of the story. When you got to shore...?

**Peter:** *(Turning to the congregation and pantomiming.)* When we got to shore we saw a campfire, and Jesus had breakfast going for us. It seemed just like old times. We took him a few of the fish — *(emphasizing)* the 153 fish! — and he broiled them on the charcoal, and brought them around to each of us, and we all ate until we were stuffed. Nothing is so good as breakfast on the shore.

**John:** *(Looking at Peter seriously.)* So? Are we going to tell the rest of the story? Or shall we just leave it at this?

**Peter:** *(Thoughtfully pausing, rubbing his head and wincing — then nodding.)* We should tell the rest. *(He indicates to the Reader to continue.)*

**Reader:** John 21:15-16. *(He stops to address Peter.)* Why did he ask you the second time, Peter? Did he not hear you the first time?

**Peter:** *(Looking at the Reader, and shaking his head sadly.)* No, Sir. He had a reason. In fact, he asked me a *third* time, "Simon, son of John, do you love me?" *(Turns back to the worshipers.)* I have to admit, it hurt my feelings to be asked the same thing three times. He already *knew* that I loved him. But I think it was his way of countering those — *(shakes his head sadly and takes a deep breath)* those three terrible denials I had made at the high priest's house that night. Each time he asked, it was like he was saying, "Say what you should have said that night, Peter." *(Shows three fingers.)* Three times I denied it — and three times I confessed my love. It was hard, but I needed to do it — to move on beyond that nightmare — to get on with his work.

**John:** *(Admiringly to Peter.)* And you have, Buddy. You've gotten on with it, and I'm proud of you. The Lord is proud of you. You're the man! I know, because I'm the guy who wrote it all down.

**Reader:** *(To John.)* And we are forever in your debt, Sir. *(Then to Peter.)* And in yours, Friend. We thank you both. *(Peter and John exit the nearest door as the song begins.)*

**Congregational Song:** "Dear Lord And Father Of Mankind" or "Higher Ground"

### Fifth Sunday After Easter
### Matthew: The Commissioning And Ascension
### Acts 1:4-11; Matthew 28:16-20

*(Matthew comes in quickly just after the service begins, and moves to a seat which has been reserved for him in a very central part of the congregation. If in biblical dress, he wears a dark tunic similar to a friar's frock, and his head is uncovered. Add a simple sash and sandals. On one shoulder he totes an **open leather satchel filled with several scrolls**, made from brown postal wrap affixed to simple dowels.)*

**Reader:** This morning our scripture will pick up in the middle of a familiar story which happened at the end of the forty days Jesus remained on earth following his resurrection. The Apostles and the women had returned to Jerusalem area. We find them meeting with Jesus just outside the city, near Bethany in the Olivet Range. I will begin reading from Acts 1:6. **Acts 1:6-8.**

**Matthew:** *(Standing quickly and speaking loudly from his place.)* I was there! I was with Jesus that day, Sir!

**Reader:** *(Stopping to find the voice, and asking.)* You were there on the mountain that day? And who, Sir, might you be?

**Matthew:** I am one of the Twelve, Matthew. You may have heard of the book I wrote about the life of Jesus.

**Reader:** *(Smiling warmly.)* Yes, Sir, we certainly have. Congregation, we are honored this morning to have the Apostle Matthew as our guest. *(He leads in a welcoming applause.)* And we would be so honored to have you help us with this story, Sir.

**Matthew:** *(Looking through his satchel of scrolls.)* I have the notes on that day right here — in one of these scrolls. I always kept good notes on all the things Jesus told us. Never can tell when you might need to check — Yes, here! *(He pulls out a scroll and opens it, looking for something.)* That was when Jesus told us about the power.

**Reader:** *(Looking somewhat puzzled.)* The power, Sir? Tell us about the power.

**Matthew:** *(Referring to the scroll.)* Jesus said, "Do not leave Jerusalem, but wait for the gift my Father promised, which you have heard me speak about. For John baptized with water, but in a few days you will be baptized with the Holy Spirit."

**Reader:** *(Nodding assent.)* Yes — *that* Power — the Spirit of God.

**Matthew:** *(Still referring to the scroll.)* And there is more. Then Jesus said, "You shall receive power when the Holy Spirit comes on you; and you will be my witnesses in Jerusalem, and in all Judea and Samaria, and to the ends of the earth." *(Now re-rolling the scroll and putting it back into the satchel as he speaks.)* But, I have more. I included this in the book I wrote also, and I remembered even more that he said at that time. *(He searches through the collection of scrolls again, eventually bringing up another one.)*

**Reader:** *(As Matthew is searching.)* I think we would know that as the Great Commission, in Matthew 28:18-20. That is probably the most familiar paragraph in your book to us, Sir. We would be honored for you to read it to us.

**Matthew:** *(Opening the new scroll, searching it quickly, then reading.)* Yes, here it is. **Matthew 28:16.**

**Reader:** *(Interrupting.)* But, Sir, you said it happened in Galilee, and the other account clearly said near Bethany in the Olivet Range. I wonder why the difference?

**Matthew:** Oh — easy to explain. Jesus said these words several times. John remembers him giving us the commission and the power in the upper room, that first evening after he was resurrected. And in the Acts story it was said near Bethany — which was the last time. My story recalls a time between, while we were still in Galilee.

**Reader:** *(Looking agreeable.)* Perhaps the words were so very important, Jesus said them over in different places for emphasis?

**Matthew:** *(Nodding agreement.)* Jesus often did that — repeated important truths so we would grasp and remember them. I'll continue ... *(reading from the scroll again)* **Matthew 28:17-20.**

**Reader:** Those are daunting words, Friend. How were they received by his men?

**Matthew:** *(Re-rolling the scroll thoughtfully, and holding it.)* Very seriously, I would say. We realized he was finally going away. And we would be left alone to finish what he had begun in our three years together. Without the Power — *(shakes his head)* without the Power it just could not be done.

**Reader:** And what is that power, Sir? How would you define it?

**Matthew:** *(Tightly grasping the scroll and using it to emphasize each word as he answers.)* We came to realize that the Power, Brother, is the Presence — the Presence of Jesus himself within us. Did you hear his final words? "I am with you always, to the very end of the age." That promise remains in effect, in the Holy Spirit of Jesus, living in our hearts. It is by that Power we witness and serve.

**Reader:** *(Referring back to the Bible.)* I am still looking at the story as told in the book of Acts, chapter 1. It continues like this. *(He reads.)* **Acts 1:9.**

**Matthew:** *(Nodding, remembering.)* Oh, yes! We were standing there with our mouths agape, *(indicates upward)* watching him go up in an awesome mix of joy and fear. Losing him was more than we could bear, yet knowing he would be with us in his Spirit gave us relief and joy about our future. So we just stood there *(pantomimes the expression, looking upward)* somewhat agog.

**Reader:** *(Referring once more to Acts.)* And then it says ... *(reading)* **Acts 1:10-11.** *(To Matthew.)* Was that not even more cause for joy, Friend? That Jesus would one day return?

**Matthew:** Oh, yes, Sir! Yes it was! And yes it *is!* *(Turns to the congregation.)* We haven't seen the end of things yet, people. Jesus is coming back! But meanwhile, he has given all of us his work to do. *(Pointing with the scroll to the two Pentecost banners.)* Receive the Power of Jesus' Spirit. Then tell everyone around you the Good News! *(Matthew takes his seat.)*

**Reader:** Thank you, Matthew. Folks, it sounds like we have work to do!

**Congregational Song:** "Share His Love" or "So Send I You"

## Sixth Sunday After Easter
## Jesus' Mother Mary and Salome: Praying With Joy
## Luke 24:50-53 and Acts 1:12-26

*(Mary and Salome enter together just before the service begins, and take seats on the center aisle, about two-thirds of the way back. Both ladies wear simple, unbelted tunics in gray or neutral colors, and sandals. Each has a veil wrapped around her head and shoulders. Mary's is a deep purple, and Salome's a black or dark gray. Each may also wear or carry a shawl or wrap of black monks cloth or similar woven fabric. They are quiet as the service begins, except for looking around with amazement at the worship room, and occasionally sharing a whisper about something they have discovered in it.)*

**Reader:** *(Not recognizing the women yet.)* Today we continue our readings of the events which took place between Jesus' resurrection and the day of Pentecost. Pentecost, also called The Feast of Weeks by the Jews, was a celebration of the early harvest. God commanded to Moses that it be celebrated fifty days after the Passover and Unleavened Bread observance. When forty of the fifty days had passed, Jesus met with his followers a last time to commission them, and was then taken back to heaven. At the instruction of angels, the group had turned from the Mount of Olives, and started back for the now-familiar upper room in Jerusalem. Let me read: **Luke 24:50-53 and Acts 1:12-15.**

*(As the reading progresses, Mary and Salome become very interested, then excited, pointing to the Reader and whispering loudly.)*

**Mary:** *(As the Acts scripture begins, they speak in stage whispers, becoming low voice, creating a little disturbance in their pew.)* Why, we were there, Salome! *(Salome nods and responds.)* We know this story — that man is talking about us! *(Pointing to each other.)* About the day Jesus left to return to his father! And about the angels! Listen — he mentioned my name! He mentioned me by name!

**Reader:** *(Noticing the women's agitation, he pauses to listen, and then calls to them.)* You ladies seem to know about these things. What would you share with us to help us understand?

**Mary:** *(Stops talking to Salome and looks to the Reader, then hesitantly stands.)* Sir, pardon the interruption, but that story you were reading — it sounds like one that happened to me — *(includes Salome)* to us.

**Reader:** I was reading about the ten days after Jesus' ascension and before Pentecost, when his followers returned to Jerusalem to wait and pray.

**Mary:** *(Excited.)* Yes! Yes! Salome and I were there with them in prayer during those days.

**Reader:** Well, welcome, ladies. Would you tell us your names, please?

**Salome:** *(Standing beside Mary, pointing to herself.)* My name is Salome. You might know me better as James and John's mother. *(Touching Mary's sleeve.)* And this is my sister, Mary. I think you know her already as the mother of our Lord. *(The women look at each other quickly,* *and Salome continues.)* We were just excited to hear you tell about those days in Jerusalem, before the promise of the Holy Spirit came true.

**Reader:** Yes, thank you so much. We welcome you both, and I would like to ask a question about that scripture we just heard. What did you *do* during those ten days — besides pray, I mean? *(Gestures with empty hands and a shrug.)* Or did you pray the entire ten days?

*(The women look at each other, deciding who will answer. Salome motions to Mary, and sits back down, watching Mary as she speaks.)*

**Mary:** Oh, we were so full of joy that day! I can't tell you, there are so many reasons. *(Grasps her index finger as she begins to count the reasons.)* Seeing Jesus always brought joy — to all of us, but especially to me. *(Adds a second finger.)* Knowing he was alive and well, and returning to his True Father — that was full circle for me. God had sent him to us — to Joseph and me — and now he was calling him back to his rightful glory. I could not be sad to see him leave, knowing he would be honored in the heavenly realms so greatly.

**Reader:** That would make a mother's heart joyful!

**Mary:** *(Adding a third finger.)* But then there was the promise — the promise that he would return again to us just as he had gone away. Oh, the very thought of seeing Jesus again made us very happy, whether in this life, or in the next.

**Reader:** That we *can* understand, Mary. We all look forward to that wonderful day when Jesus comes back for us. But what about the work? *(Points to his Bible.)* Jesus gave such a huge task to all of you — to take the Good News about him into the entire world. Were you not a little frightened by that?

**Mary:** Oh — but did you not hear the other promise? The one about his power and his Spirit?

**Reader:** *(A little embarrassed.)* Oh, yes, but we read that last week, when we met Matthew. Yes! The promise of power.

**Mary:** Well, I could not say we were not overwhelmed by the mission, but our fear was offset by knowing Jesus would come to us in his Spirit — in some way. *(Shakes her head slightly, wondering.)* We didn't know how that would happen, *(nods brightly)* but we did know it would come. Jesus always kept his word.

**Salome:** *(Tugging gently on Mary's sleeve.)* But, Sister, answer the question. He asked what we did for those ten days. Remember? We prayed and went to the Temple and all that.

**Mary:** *(Nodding thanks.)* Yes, that is what we did, Sir. We spent ten joyful days in anticipation, going to the Temple for the hours of prayer each day, talking to people about Jesus' resurrection, and waiting for the Promise.

**Salome:** *(Tugging her sleeve again.)* And we chose Matthias to replace Judas.

**Mary:** *(Nods to Salome again.)* Oh, yes! Matthias.

**Reader:** Yes, that follows in the next verses. *(Reads.)* **Acts 1:14-17 and 21-23.**

**Mary:** *(Nodding vigorously as she listens.)* Yes, they cast the lots, and Matthias was chosen. A good man. It seemed important to Peter and some of the others to have that twelfth place filled again. To be able to move on, I guess. They were quite disappointed in Judas.

**Salome:** *(Echoing, gesturing to the Reader.)* Made it seem complete, you know.

**Reader:** *(Nods.)* We thank you ladies for helping us with this story. *(He leads the congregation in a polite applause, and both ladies stand and gesture their thanks.)* We are glad to know those were not ten days of fear for you. Or a time of anguished prayer, blaming yourselves for Jesus' death. It helps to know that it was a season of *joy*, because that is what we want our lives with Jesus to be today — lives of *joyful* anticipation of blessings to come.

**Mary:** *(Agreeing.)* You know, before he died, Jesus told us, *(emphasizes by pointing her index finger)* "I tell you the truth, you will weep and mourn while the world rejoices. You will grieve, *but your grief will turn to joy.*" Jesus wanted us to have joy — his joy — his abundant life. He was a man of joy, that Son of mine. *(She sits beside Salome again.)*

**Congregational Song:** "Wonderful, Wonderful Jesus" or "O Happy Day That Fixed My Choice"

<br>

### Pentecost Sunday
### Peter: The Power Comes
### Acts 2:1-47

*(Peter is in a long tunic, with head square and turban, all of natural-colored fabrics. He wears sandals on bare feet, and has a belt of rope. As the service begins, he enters at the back, and stands behind the worshipers, waiting and listening.)*

**Reader:** At last the day we have waited for is here — Pentecost Sunday — and the story of the coming of God's promised Holy Spirit in power on the Believers. Let me begin the reading. **Acts 2:1-4.** *(He places his hand on the Bible and looks up wistfully.)* Oh — that we might have been there that day — to see it, and hear it, and *feel* it! It must have been so real!

**Peter:** *(Starts forward briskly as the pastor looks up from his reading, reaching almost to the front as he begins speaking.)* Oh, Brother — I wish that for you, too! *(Gestures to include all the congregation.)* For all of you. I was there! I was there! And it was a day so awesome I cannot even describe it to you.

**Reader:** *(Recognizing Peter from week 4.)* Peter! Welcome back! There could be no better person to tell us about that historic day!

**Peter:** *(Comes onto the platform, shakes the Reader's hand, gives an embrace, and begins to speak.)* All of us were together that day.

**Reader:** *(Interrupting.)* How many were there, Peter?

**Peter:** *(Acknowledging the Reader kindly.)* Probably most of the 120 or so Believers, Friend. *(Then continuing.)* We were all together for the feast day — it was Pentecost, as you have said. The city was very crowded *(sweeping gesture)* because the feast falls in late spring, and the weather is good for travel. The Law commands that no labor be done that day, so everyone was free to come for the celebration.

*(Pauses, listening.)* Then — suddenly — drowning us out with its roar — came the sound of an almost tornadic wind. And with it *(pauses again, looking upward, pointing as though following a flying object)* just as suddenly — everyone saw it — tongues of fire, breaking apart and seeming to rest *(touches the crown of his head)* on each Believer's head. We heard it — then we saw it — but mostly we *felt* it! Something came over us, overwhelmed us, took control of us. Even the house was trembling!

*(Pauses again, remembering.)* And then we knew! *(He makes a tight fist for emphasis.)* It had to be the Power of Jesus — *(gestures as a dove descending from heaven to his chest)* the Spirit of our Lord returning to be with us, and to live *in* us. I guess we all just began to pour out of that upper room and into the streets, shouting and praising God. It was an awesome sense of joy, knowing that the Lord was keeping his word to us. That the Power had come.

**Reader:** *(He listens thoughtfully to Peter's story, then responds.)* What a wonder to have been there. *(Points to his Bible.)* It says here that pilgrims were listening and understanding from all over the world. *(Reads again.)* **Acts 2:5-13.** *(To Peter with amused surprise.)* They thought you were drunk?

**Peter:** *(Laughing at the question.)* I guess we were pretty happy, and just a bit noisy. And we were talking sounds that were gibberish to some of them. But quickly we got our wits about us, and I found a high place to stand and get their attention. I told them, "These folks aren't drunk, as you suppose. No! You are witnessing the fulfilling of the words of the prophet Joel...."

**Reader:** *(Interrupting.)* I have that quote right here, Peter. Let me read it for you. **Acts 2:17-18 and 21.** It fell on everyone, didn't it? Men and women, young and old. Everyone was a prophet that day!

**Peter:** *(Nods and continues, excited at the memory.)* Then I went on and explained to them about Jesus. How he lived and worked miracles, and how they had killed him. *(Hammers his fist into his palm.)* Crucified God's Son and Messiah! But *(lifts hands to the sky)* God had raised him to life! That's the important part — that he came back to life.

**Reader:** *(Motioning to his Bible, and reading.)* **Acts 2:22-24 and 32.**

**Peter:** *(Listening, nodding strong agreement.)* And then we gave the invitation, and, Pastor, you would have been amazed at the response. I told them, *(gestures broadly across the audience)*

"Repent and be baptized, every one of you, in the name of Jesus Christ, for the forgiveness of your sins. *(Gestures down from heaven to his chest.)* And you will receive the Holy Spirit." And they began to come up and ask us — all twelve of us — to pray with them, and explain to them. And we baptized many of them that very day!

**Reader:** *(Shaking his head at the incredible story.)* The story ends like this: **Acts 2:41-42.** *(To Peter.)* And that was just the beginning of it, wasn't it?

**Peter:** *(Nods and shakes his head, almost in disbelief.)* We just kept on growing, and people kept on being saved. We grew *(gestures the size with hands growing wider apart)* to 5,000, and then to 10,000; and many of the Jewish priests and leaders even believed and joined with us. *(Shakes his head again.)* I tell you, when Jesus said, "Power," he meant *Power!* We truly saw it in all its glory on that day! *(To the congregation.)* Folks, I tell you, never doubt what God can do when the time is right. It could happen again. It could happen to you. *(To the Reader and Pastor.)* Thank you, Brothers, for letting me share with you. It thrills my heart to tell it again. It was the greatest day of my life! *(Peter embraces them and exits though the nearest door.)*

**Congregational Song:** "Breathe On Me" or "To God Be The Glory"

CPSIA information can be obtained at www.ICGtesting.com
Printed in the USA
BVOW06s1935090714

358575BV00016B/212/P

9 780788 019937